BATTLEFIELD
WALKS
THE SOUTH

David Clark

Grange
BOOKS

A Sutton Publishing Book

This edition published in 1997 by Grange Books
An imprint of Grange Books plc
The Grange
Grange Yard
London SE1 3AG

ISBN 1-84013-009-1

This book was designed and produced by
Alan Sutton Publishing Limited, an imprint of Sutton Publishing Limited,
Phoenix Mill, Thrupp, Stroud, Gloucestershire, GL5 2BU

Typeset in 11/12 Ehrhardt.
Typesetting and origination by
Sutton Publishing Limited.
Printed in Great Britain by
WBC Limited, Bridgend.

CONTENTS

Introduction   v

 1   The Battle of Ashdown   1

 2   The Battle of Maldon   12

 3   The Battle of Hastings   24

 4   The Battle of Lewes   37

 5   The Battle of Barnet   50

 6   The Battle of Lansdown   63

 7   The Siege of Gloucester   75

 8   The First Battle of Newbury   87

 9   The Battle of Cheriton   99

10   The Battle of Langport   111

11   The Battle of Sedgemoor   122

12   RAF Charmy Down   137

Further Reading   148

Index   151

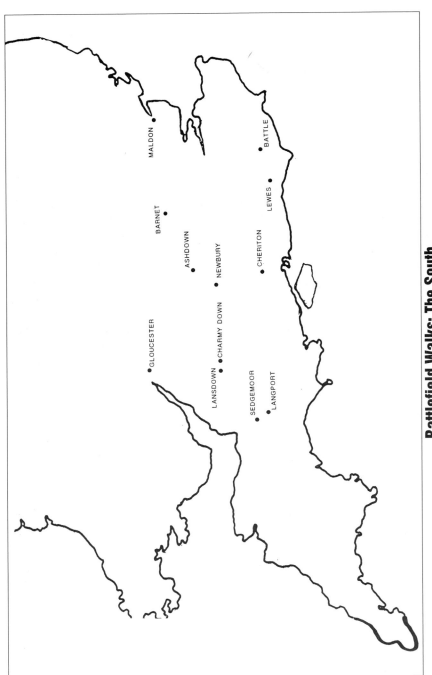

MALDON

BATTLE

BARNET

LEWES

ASHDOWN

NEWBURY

CHERITON

GLOUCESTER

CHARMY DOWN

LANSDOWN

SEDGEMOOR

LANGPORT

Battlefield Walks: The South

INTRODUCTION

Allowing for notable exceptions, much of the warfare which has taken place on English soil may be attributed to the two great civil wars: the Wars of the Roses (1455–1487) and the English Civil Wars (1642–1651). However, none of the many battles fought in the south of England during the English Civil Wars were of the utmost significance, with the Midlands (Edgehill and Naseby) and the North (Marston Moor) providing the venues for the most celebrated engagements. Similarly, decisive battles of the Wars of the Roses tended to be staged in the North (Towton) and Midlands (Bosworth). For important battles in the South, one has to travel further back in time. And the journey is well worth it.

For example, the Battle of Ashdown (871) showed that the Saxons could fight the Danes and win, the Saxon victory owing much to the young Alfred. The Battle of Hastings (1066), while demonstrating that they could fight the Normans and lose, brought about major changes that destroyed England's insularity and ushered in the process which would one day result in European unity. And Simon de Montfort's victory at the Battle of Lewes (1264) enabled him to convene the very first Parliament, putting England on the long road to present-day Parliamentary democracy.

The South of England also staged the last major battle to take place on English soil: the Battle of Sedgemoor (1685), the culmination of a rebellion which had as its aftermath a savage blood-letting forever to be associated with the name of Judge Jeffreys. This volume also includes explorations of six Civil War battlesites, including Lansdown (1643), Cheriton (1644) and Langport (1645), which although perhaps not of the first rank in terms of importance certainly do offer most attractive walks.

On the whole, the walks might be described as short, but they may also cover relatively demanding terrain. Lewes and Lansdown, for example, involve the negotiation of some steep hills, while ramblers on Sedgemoor may find the going quite heavy in wet weather. And although the suggested walks should be enjoyable in their own right, it must be remembered that progress may be hindered by a desire to follow the course of a battle in one's imagination.

As far as peripheral information is concerned, an attempt has been made to smooth the visitor's path. Motorists are provided with advice about the best roads of approach and about car parking facilities at each site. In some instances, it may be more convenient to travel by train and the railway stations at Newbury, Gloucester and Hastings (Battle) are all in close proximity to the suggested walks. Whenever possible, in order to derive the full benefit from a visit, it is a good idea to arrange a weekend trip – which will also render it possible to take in a selection of the suggested destinations for further explorations.

All the walks are circular, which means that they can be picked up at any point along the way, and, wherever possible, routes have been designed to take in at least one public house. Recommended reading, which ideally should be undertaken before a walk, is restricted to books that are generally available via the public library system. A visit to the appropriate Tourist Office can also be useful in terms of the acquisition of relevant leaflets and street plans, although it must be added that staff knowledge of local battlefields is often rather limited.

The prime aim of this book is to provide the reader with information which will enhance visits to the battlefields of southern England. However, at the time of writing (1995) discussions are taking place about a planned by-pass which may well impair the quality of a visit to the site of the First Battle of Newbury (see pp 87–98). As this is only one of several battlefields which is currently under threat from developments of one form or another throughout the country, a concomitant aim must be to raise public awareness of a worrying national trend. With everything from modest town walks to more demanding country walks, I hope that there will be something of interest for everyone, and that the book itself will stimulate interest in battlefields and in the continuing fight necessary to preserve both the sites themselves and reasonable public access to them.

1
THE BATTLE OF ASHDOWN
8 January 871

Introduction

During the period of its lengthy decline, the Roman Empire gradually lost the ability to defend its outlying provinces. After the Roman departure from Britain in the early years of the fifth century, the Britons found themselves being pushed further and further west by the Angles, Saxons and Jutes. Initially, these invaders contented themselves with lightning attacks along the east coast. Occasionally, there would be a large scale raid in which they were assisted by the Picts and the Irish – who would continue to offer their support to all would-be invaders for the next 1,300 years. The loss of an efficient Roman central administration led to squabbling between several tribal chieftains, who preferred fighting among themselves to presenting a united front against the threat of invasion. The prospective settlers lacked the organization and resources of their Roman predecessors, but were able to establish a bridgehead in Kent in AD 449 when the powerful Briton, Voltigern, gave the Isle of Thanet to the Germanic *émigré*, Hengist, in exchange for military aid. As soon as he was strong enough, Hengist turned on his patron and took Kent for himself. Similar developments occurred in Sussex and on the eastern seaboard from the Wash to the Humber.

The advance was checked temporarily by Ambrosius Aurelianus, a survivor of the Roman occupation, and latterly by Artorius, who has been identified with the legendary King Arthur. It is thought that both commanders' successes depended on the effective deployment of cavalry against which the Saxons, who invariably fought on foot, were at a pronounced disadvantage. It was to this period that the Battle of Mount Badon belongs. Fought between AD 490 and AD 516, at an unidentified location, the encounter ended in victory for Artorius, and secured a temporary reprieve for the Britons. Yet it proved impossible to dislodge the newcomers from their established strongholds and the process of Anglo-Saxon settlement and to an extent integration with the indigent Britons went on.

Gradually the map of England began to show the development of three power-blocs: Northumbria, stretching northwards from the Humber; Wessex, covering southern England south of the Thames; and, between these two, the 'middle-England' of Mercia. Conflict between the three and, indeed, within each kingdom, meant that boundaries were subject to continuous change, but each, in turn, enjoyed a period of unrivalled supremacy. First, during the seventh century, Northumbria grew to prominence under King Edwin, who had been converted to Christianity. Edwin was killed in battle by the heathen, Penda of Mercia, who displayed Edwin's head at York, thus beginning a ghoulish tradition among conquerors that survived for several centuries. Edwin's successor, Oswald, met a similar fate at Penda's hands before Penda himself was defeated in battle by Oswald's younger brother, Oswy, whose victory both sustained Northumbria's position and helped to establish the Christian faith more widely.

Eventually divisions within Northumbria destroyed the stability of the kingdom, allowing Mercia, under Ethelbald and Offa, to become the dominant power in the eighth century. Offa became recognized, even more so than Edwin in earlier years, as the King of all England, in which capacity he took his place in European society. The lasting monument to his power, etched into the landscape, was Offa's Dyke, an earthwork running for 120 miles along the border between England and Wales. Whereas Edwin's overlordship had been based on strong government, however, Offa's dominance was built on fear. With his death, Mercian power waned, ushering in a period of expansion for Wessex, which had been deprived of much territory as a result of Offa's incursions. It would fall to the kings of Wessex, and one king in particular, to lead English resistance to a new and terrible threat from without.

The Road to Ashdown

The supremacy of Wessex was established by King Egbert, grandfather of Alfred the Great, through his victory over the Mercians at the Battle of Ellandun in 825. His territorial gains, including present-day Berkshire, Sussex, Kent and Essex, transformed Wessex into a superpower, capable of taking on the most formidable foe.

An enemy worthy of this description had visited England in 793, pillaging the holy community on the island of Lindisfarne. The culprits, Danish raiders, popularly known as Vikings, made no further raids until 835, after which attacks of increasing duration and depth of penetration became the norm, year after year. Driven by the need for new lands to settle, coupled with the impetus provided by a naturally belligerent temperament, the Danes appeared to the Saxons much as the Saxons themselves had appeared to the Britons: ruthless and unstoppable.

To begin with, the Danish menace was limited to swift, uncoordinated coastal raids. Occasionally, as in 851, a more substantial raiding party would spend the winter in England, but the real business of conquest did not begin until 865 when an army converged on East Anglia. In 866, with the Northumbrians engaged in a civil war, they marched swiftly on York. By the time Northumbrian differences were patched up, the Danes had become so well entrenched that a Saxon attempt to re-take York in the spring of 867 ended in defeat. Before moving on to pastures new, the invaders were able to place a puppet king on the Northumbrian throne.

Their next objective was Mercia. The Mercians asked their one-time enemies, the men of Wessex, for assistance. Egbert of Wessex had died in 839 and was succeeded by his son, Ethelwulf, who himself had four sons: Ethelbald, Ethelbert, Ethelred and Alfred, all of whom ruled in turn. Ethelred, who had succeeded to the throne in 866, hastened to the aid of Mercia, attacking the Danes as they were digging in at Nottingham. Had the Mercians held firm, the Danish master-plan might have faltered. Instead, they sued for peace, leaving Ethelred to struggle home. Too late did the Mercians and East Angles come to realize the futility of attempting to make a lasting peace, both kingdoms being subjected to pillage and wanton destruction.

After the encounter with Ethelred at Nottingham, the invaders retired to York, where they remained for a further twelve months, after which they were ready to carry the gospel of death into Wessex. At Thetford, they crushed an East Anglian army before making their way up the Thames to Reading, which they occupied towards the end of 870. A foraging party sent out from Reading was challenged at Englefield by Ethelwulf, the local alderman, and put to flight. A few days later, Ethelwulf was joined by King Ethelred and his young brother, Alfred. This combined Saxon force laid siege to the town, but was surprised by a sudden attack, as the Danes charged out of their stronghold and into the Saxon camp. Despite putting up a brave resistance, the Saxons were forced to retreat, leaving Ethelwulf dead on the field.

It is said that the Saxons, shamed by this defeat, actively sought a further engagement, but it seems more probable that they were forced into a second battle sooner than was convenient for them when the Danes, sensing an opportunity to bring the conquest of Wessex to an early and successful conclusion, regrouped and marched out of Reading in pursuit. Having accepted the inevitability of another battle, Ethelred and Alfred halted on the Berkshire Downs to await their arrival, rather than risk being overtaken by the fast-moving marauders. The sequence of events immediately prior to the encounter is unclear, but it seems that by 7 January 871, both armies were in close proximity and making preparations for a battle on the morrow.

The Battle of Ashdown

On the morning of 8 January 871, the Danes secured an advantage by taking up a position on the lower slopes of Lowbury Hill, near the Ridgeway. There were two Danish kings, Bagseg and Halfdan, and many earls, so the army was split into two divisions, Bagseg and Halfdan contenting themselves with one wing, while the earls were given command of the other.

According to Bishop Asser's account of the engagement, written in 893 on the basis of information supplied by participants, Alfred reached the field ahead of Ethelred who was determined to hear mass before going into battle – refusing to budge until his devotional preparations were complete. The Saxon strategy had been to follow the Danish lead by dividing their own force, with Ethelred facing Bagseg and Halfdan, and Alfred taking on the Danish earls. Unfortunately, Ethelred's non-appearance rendered his brother's position untenable, forcing Alfred to advance on the Danish shield-wall alone, although he still proceeded according to the original plan. Bishop Asser is anxious to point out that Alfred, albeit with a greater sense of urgency than Ethelred, also sought 'divine counsel', before closing up the Saxon shield-wall and advancing on the enemy.

Bishop Asser, perhaps the very first explorer of British battlefields, subsequently visited the site and claimed to have seen a hawthorn tree around which the fighting took place. Hawthorns are abundant in the area today, but the Domesday Book records that the site of Asser's solitary hawthorn is at the point where the road from Aldworth crosses the

The battlefield of Ashdown. The area between the paling and Lowbury Hill – rising gently in the middle distance – was probably the scene of heavy fighting between Saxons and Danes.

Ridgeway. It must be said, however, that the Bishop's interest in the hawthorn was bound up rather more with its religious symbolism in terms of the circumstances surrounding the Saxon victory than with his desire to pinpoint the site of the battle.

At some indeterminate stage, Ethelred arrived on the scene to take his rightful place at the head of the Saxon division opposite the Danish kings. A mild mannered, devout Christian, he was nevertheless a brave warrior. It is just possible, in accordance with tradition, that he himself killed Bagseg. And yet, as far as Asser is concerned, the battle belongs to Alfred, who fought 'like a wild boar'.

At the outset, the Danes would have benefited from the impetus of a downhill charge, which they had every right to believe would break the Saxon lines. But the Saxon shield-wall remained firm. Some later sources say that the battle went on for most of the day; Asser merely states that the fighting continued 'for quite a long time'. What is certain is that the Danish divisions, perhaps after the death of Bagseg, began to wilt, eventually taking flight. The Saxons then broke lines to engage in a pursuit which went on until the next day, when the surviving Danes sought refuge in their stronghold at Reading.

A Saxon shield-wall could be well-nigh impenetrable, and the Danes had discovered that the best way to break it was to break ranks themselves. By feigning defeat, they were able to turn on their over-eager pursuers and, having gained the space necessary for wielding their favourite weapon, the battleaxe, were able to destroy their enemies in ferocious hand-to-hand combat. This stratagem required perfect timing and it may be that it was attempted at Ashdown, but went badly wrong. In addition to Bagseg, the Danes lost many men of note in the battle, including Earl Sidroc the Old, Earl Sidroc the Younger, Earl Osbern, Earl Fraena and Earl Harold. The Saxons rejoiced, as did Asser, who interpreted the battle in simple terms of the triumph of good over evil.

The Aftermath

According to Bishop Asser, only fourteen days after their victory at Ashdown, Ethelred and Alfred again took the field against the Danes at Basing. In this instance, the Danes proved their durability by trouncing what was, perhaps, a somewhat over-confident Saxon army. Two months later, another battle took place at Meretun, the exact location of which is unknown, although it is thought to have been deep in the heart of Wessex. Although the fighting was fierce and there was great loss of life on both sides, once again the Danes gained the upper hand.

Shortly afterwards, possibly as a result of wounds received at Meretun, Ethelred died and was buried at Wimborne Minster. He had reigned for the relatively short (though not unusually so for the time) period of five years. Alfred, who seems to have been regarded as heir to the throne, quickly took his brother's place. Despite leading a rapidly dwindling force, he fought on against a Danish army that had been strengthened by an influx of summer marauders. At the ensuing Battle of Wilton, following a day of heavy fighting, the Danes retreated, only to put into effect – more successfully on this occasion – their ruse of turning on their scattered pursuers and cutting them to pieces.

Considering the losses he had sustained in a year of almost continuous fighting, Alfred had little choice but to sue for peace. As soon as they were in possession of what must have been a substantial tribute, the Danes retreated to London with a view to wintering there, and it was the turn of the Mercians to raise the necessary funds to buy peace.

The peace purchased by Alfred lasted for five years. In part this may have been due to the Danes' preoccupation with affairs in Northumbria, where Egbert, their puppet king, was in the process of being overthrown. The only engagement in which Alfred is recorded as having taken part in this period is a naval one when, it is noted by Asser, he fought six or seven Danish ships, capturing one and putting the remainder to flight. Appreciative of the advantage to be gained by meeting a weary invasion fleet before it had landed, Alfred issued orders for the construction of warships throughout the kingdom.

Alfred the Great, as depicted in a thirteenth-century manuscript. (Bodleian Library)

Notwithstanding this minor setback, the Danes – of whom there seemed to be an inexhaustible supply – under Guthrum launched an unexpected mid-winter assault on the West Saxons, establishing a stronghold at Chippenham. But the biggest prize of all eluded them, for although many of his supporters were killed or reduced to slavery, Alfred himself managed to effect an escape, taking refuge in the marshes. It is to this period in Alfred's life that many of the celebrated legends of his reign belong. The most famous of these is the tale of Alfred and the bread, of which Asser, sadly, makes no mention. The story goes that, alone and friendless, Alfred had taken refuge with a swineherd and his family. Unaware of his identity, the swineherd's wife asked the king to keep an eye on some bread that she had placed in the oven. Preoccupied with weightier matters, he allowed the bread to burn – earning a well-deserved scolding.

Eventually, Alfred established a base at Athelney, from where he directed a number of successful guerilla raids against the enemy. On one occasion, according to another unsubstantiated tale, he disguised himself as a minstrel and contrived to infiltrate the Danish camp while a council of war was being held, learning much valuable information by this ruse.

Amid all his adventures, he found the time to raise a new army which assembled early in May 878. At a place identified by Asser as Egbert's Stone in Selwood Forest – possibly near Stourton – he was joined by men from Somerset, Wiltshire and Hampshire. Marching via Eastleigh Wood near Sutton Veny, the Saxons came upon the Danish army at Edington. In the ensuing battle, the Danes could not penetrate the Saxon shield-wall and were put to flight. Unable, on this occasion, to regroup, they fled to their stronghold at Chippenham. Alfred laid siege to the town and within two weeks the defenders, on the verge of starvation, surrendered. Under the Treaty of Chippenham, Guthrum's army promised to leave Wessex, withdrawing to settle in the Eastern Counties. Alfred had won his war and had saved England from total conquest.

The Walk

Distance: 5½ miles (8.9 km)

Start in the village of Compton. Close to the Swan public house are lay-bys which double as bus stops, but where one may park if driving. The lay-by on the same side of the road as the Swan has a local map indicating public rights of way in the area and is the starting point: Point A (Pathfinder 1171 520799).

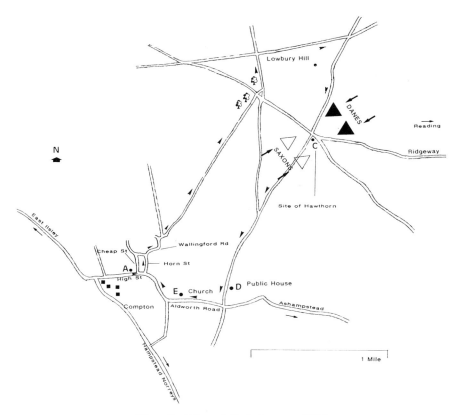

The Battle of Ashdown, 871

Walk past the Swan and turn sharp left into Horne Street. Ahead is the Baxter Health Care factory. Turn right into Wallingford Road which narrows to a track leading to Stocks Farm. However, walk under the railway bridge (Pathfinder 1155 524803) and bear left. This path soon develops into one of the broad chalk tracks for which the Berkshire Downs are famous.

On the left of the track, immediately after the turning which leads to Roden Farm, is a Roman burial ground (Pathfinder 1155 532818). It is at this point that the main body of Alfred's army probably gathered. Continue on to the woods ahead (Pathfinder 1155 534820) (Point B). Immediately before the trees, the track crosses the Ridgeway Path. Continue along the track, bearing left and skirting the lower reaches of Lowbury Hill (Pathfinder 1155 540823), the site of a Roman temple. Excavations, which revealed the burial of a middle-aged woman, suggest that the hill, which dominates the horizon, was occupied in the Iron Age. At the crossroads where the track crosses another path – the Berkshire Circular Route – turn right, so as to skirt the front of Lowbury Hill.

Ignoring two turnings to the left, keep on to the next crossroads (Pathfinder 1155 545826) and turn right, continuing along the Berkshire Circular Route and so encircling Lowbury Hill. By adhering to this track, and ignoring the minor path off to the left, one meets once more the Ridgeway Path (Pathfinder 1155 540815) (Point C). This crossroads is a possible site for the hawthorn bush mentioned in Asser's account of the battle. The Saxons would have advanced across the open ground to the right of the track with the Danes occupying the more advantageous higher ground to the left. This is where the fiercest fighting would have occurred.

This particular stretch of the route is classed as a byway open to all traffic. This is something of a bone of contention, for ramblers are always keen to draw attention to the damage wrought by cars and motorcycles. Continue along the track to the spot marked on the Pathfinder map as Crows Foot, owing to the configuration of the near-convergence of paths (Pathfinder 1155 534805). Continue straight on, downhill. The path soon develops into a single-track metalled road and Lower Farm looms up on the left. Shortly beyond the farm, there is a welcome surprise as one comes across the Red Lion public house, standing back off the road (Pathfinder 1171 530798) (Point D).

A little way further on, the track joins the road leading to Compton. Turn to the right, but take care as there is no grass verge for a short distance. On the right-hand side of the road is the Church of St Mary and St Nicholas (Pathfinder 1171 527797) (Point E) which is worth visiting. (It is necessary to stoop on entering so as to negotiate the tiny interior doorway.) Emerging from the church, walk under the railway bridge and follow the road around to the Swan Inn and the starting point.

Further Explorations

Neolithic man was probably farming the chalk uplands around 3500 BC, and the Ordnance Survey Landranger map of the area, No. 174, is liberally sprinkled with evidence of early settlement. One of the most celebrated local features is the Ridgeway Path (Landranger 174 5581) which runs for a distance of 85 miles from the Ivinghoe Beacon in Buckinghamshire to Overton Hill near Marlborough. Based upon two ancient tracks – the Ridgeway proper and the Icknield Way – it has been called the oldest highway in England, and it provided a long-distance route that was safer and firmer than the marshy plains below. Well marked, the Ridgeway looks easy to follow, but this is deceptive. The Downs are criss-crossed with footpaths, bridleways and byways of all descriptions, and landmarks to help one get one's bearings are often in short supply, so a compass is useful.

The Ridgeway, in common with many old paths, was guarded by a number of hill-forts, with earthen defences such as those at Liddington Castle (Landranger 174 2079), Uffington Castle (Landranger 174 2986) and Letcombe Regis Castle (Landranger 174 3884). At Perborough Castle (Landranger 174 5277) immediately to the south of the village of Compton, the gateway was fortified by twin towers of Saxon stone.

Place names with a connection with King Alfred include Kingstanding Hill (Landranger 174 5683) and Alfred's Castle (Landranger 174 2782), both of which have been identified as sites where Alfred pitched camp before the Battle of Ashdown. The famous Uffington White Horse (Landranger 174 3086), a 360 ft long figure of a horse cut into the chalk, may well have originated in the Iron Age. However, the Vale of the White Horse is an alternative location for the Battle of Ashdown itself, historians having debated the issue of the site of the battle as fiercely as Alfred fought the Danes. According to local tradition, after his victory Alfred's men carved out the figure of the horse to commemorate the event. Fittingly, perhaps, Berkshire was Alfred's early home, for he was born in Wantage (Landranger 174 3987), only a few miles from the site of his most celebrated victory. A statue of this great national hero stands in the market place.

As might be expected, the landscape is littered with evidence of burials in the form of barrows or tumuli, for it was the custom of Celts and Saxons to bury their dead along the Ridgeway. Examples may be seen on Lattin Down (Landranger 174 4084), Blewbury Down (Landranger 174 5282) and, most spectacularly, Lambourne Downs, where an imposing cluster of tumuli known as the 'Seven Barrows' may be seen (Landranger 174 3282). The title is somewhat misleading because this area was once a large cemetery containing about forty barrows. The barrow to the north of Sevenbarrows House and to the east of the minor road leading up to Kingston Lisle (Landranger 174 325833) was one of a number excavated and restored during the 1850s. The primary burial was of the Early Bronze Age and, in addition to further secondary burials, no less than 112 cremation burials were located in the upper levels of the barrow.

Other odd topographical features include 'Grim's Ditch', which appears at intervals along the Ridgeway (Landranger 174 4585 and Landranger 174 5383). Several Iron Age earthworks – possibly marking tribal boundaries – share this name, although they do not belong to the same system. And finally, Dragon Hill (Landranger 174 3086), near the White Horse is said to be the spot where St George slew the dragon, no grass ever having grown on the top of the hill where the monster's poisonous blood flowed.

Two miles to the south of Compton is the village Hampstead Norreys (Landranger 174 5276). Having led a somewhat sheltered existence for many centuries, the inhabitants were astonished to find themselves at the forefront of operations during the Second World War when Bomber Command established an airfield on its outskirts (Landranger 174 5477). It was a curious choice of location as the main runway terminated in dense woodland. Nevertheless, it played an important role as a base from which Wellington bombers were ferried overseas and attracted considerable attention from the Luftwaffe. Only scant evidence of the airfield remains, although it is still possible to walk across it on public footpaths.

Further Information

The village of Compton lies off the A34 between Didcot and Junction 13 of the M4. Lay-by car parking is available in High Street. Compton used to have its own railway station, on the Didcot–Southampton line, a product of 'railway mania'. One would imagine that passenger traffic along the Didcot–Newbury section was never more than light. Today, rail travellers must expect to experience the usual problems in journeying to an isolated rural location. The nearest station is Goring & Streatley on the Oxford–Reading line. Alternatively, aim for either Newbury or Reading and take a bus on to Compton. For details of rail services from London (Paddington) to Reading and Newbury, telephone 0171 262 6767. For details of National Express coach services to both destinations, call 0990 808080. Timetable information relating to local bus services to Compton from Reading and Newbury may be obtained by telephoning 01734 234524.

Further reading is limited. Ralph Whitlock's *Warrior Kings of Saxon England* (Moonraker Press, 1977) provides a useful background. An essential text is Asser's *Life of King Alfred,* an edited version of which by Simon Keynes and Michael Lapidge is grouped with other contemporary sources (Penguin, 1983). Short accounts of the battle are also to be found in David Smurthwaite's *Battlefields of Britain* and in Neil Fairbairn's *A Traveller's Guide to the Battlefields of Britain.* Ordnance Survey maps of the area are Landranger 174 and Pathfinder 1155. A complete guide to the Ridgeway long-distance footpath is Neil Curtis's *National Trail Guide: The Ridgeway* (Aurum Press, 1994).

2
THE BATTLE OF MALDON
991

Introduction

King Alfred the Great had been the Danes' most worthy adversary since the era of Charlemagne, but the Norsemen would have been mistaken if they thought that Alfred's death meant that they could step up their activities without fear of reprisal. Alfred's eldest son, Edward, while lacking his father's scholarly inclinations, may well have matched his reputation as a man of action. About thirty years of age at the time of his accession, he was a seasoned campaigner, having played a leading role in the defence of the kingdom during the harrowing raids of 892 and 893, and the West Saxons were happy to accept him as king.

Edward's accession was not entirely straightforward, however, for according to the rights of primogeniture, the two sons of Alfred's elder brother Ethelred had a far stronger claim to the throne than Edward. The elder of these two boys, Ethelwulf, appeared to accept the situation, but the younger boy, Ethelwald, entertained reservations – to the extent of occupying Wimborne before fleeing to Northumbria, where he made a pact with the resident Danes. In 902 Ethelwulf himself led a Danish raiding party into Wessex, but was killed, although his force trounced Edward's troops.

His position now unchallenged, Edward was free to continue his father's work of establishing fortresses capable of withstanding Danish attacks. Sometimes, as at Towcester in Northamptonshire, stone was used to fortify a raised earthwork, while in other locations, for example where stone was in short supply, timber was the material used. This system of defensive fortifications could also be utilized as a springboard from which to launch assaults on the southern Danelaw, and during the next twenty years Edward, working closely with his sister, Ethelfleda of Mercia, gradually pushed back the Danelaw frontier as far as the River Humber, a process helped by the defeat of the Northumbrian Danes at a battle near Tettenhall in Staffordshire in 910.

When Edward died in 924 he was succeeded by his eldest son, Athelstan, who proved to be just as capable a military commander as his father and grandfather. Edward's push into the Danelaw north of the Humber had been checked temporarily by the powerful Danish leader Ragnald, who had firmly established himself in York. By a combined strategy of diplomacy and, when necessary, use of force, Athelstan brought much of the north country to heel. The high point of his reign, and perhaps of the House of Wessex, came in 937 when he overcame an army of Scots, Irish and Danes at Brunanburgh – possibly near Rotherham – to bring a measure of national unity to the British Isles.

Athelstan reigned for fifteen years and was succeeded by his brother, Edmund, whose reign promised much. Although compelled initially to cede much of the territory Edward had conquered, by 942 he had won it back. Unfortunately, his career was cut short when he was killed in a scuffle with a thief. Edmund's infant sons, Edwy and Edgar, were passed over in favour of his brother, Edred, who took the throne. His reign was also a short one, consisting largely of renewed Saxon efforts at pacifying the north, which brought Edred into conflict with the formidable Norseman, Eric Bloodaxe. A man whose brutality was too much even for his own countrymen, Eric aimed to carve out a kingdom for himself in England, and Edred did not finally put paid to his ambitions until 954.

As with Edmund, Edred's career was cut short, his ten-year reign being terminated by illness. He was succeeded by Edmund's sons, Edwy – still a teenager when he assumed the throne – who reigned for four years, and Edgar, who reigned from 959 to 975. These were relatively peaceful years, for the famous warrior kings Alfred, Edward, Athelstan, Edmund and Edred had done their work well, enabling both Edwy and Edgar to indulge themselves in the pleasures of the flesh, in the knowledge that the kingdom was safe and their situations secure.

The Road to Maldon

However wise and firm a king may be, he needs time to establish himself among his people, and it was unfortunate for both the Wessex dynasty and the kingdom that Edgar's eldest son, Edward, reigned for only three and a half years. Edward was Edgar's son by a union which pre-dated that of his marriage to Elfrida, who had given birth to Ethelred. Elfrida would naturally have preferred to see Ethelred on the throne and it is probable that she engineered Edward's murder in 978, thus facilitating Ethelred's own coronation a year later.

Denmark and Norway had by this time become united into a single kingdom, and the Danes and Norwegians decided to test the mettle of the new boy king by mounting a few choice raids. In 980 raiding parties plundered Southampton and much of the West Country. In 982 London was pillaged. Perhaps as a result of locally raised tribute, a few comparatively quiet years followed before the raids began once more in 987.

A leading light among the later raiders was the Norwegian folk hero, Olaf Tryggvason, a veteran of raids in the Baltic, who could well have been present at the Battle of Maldon. He may even have been in command. His reputation as a warrior was legendary, his adeptness at cleaving an opponent's head in half with the aid of a hand-axe having earned him the admiration of many a fair lady. Olaf's protagonist at Maldon was a local alderman, Britnoth by name, who had also acquired a reputation as a fighting man. While Olaf was yet in the prime of life, Britnoth had attained his sixty-fifth year – quite a ripe old age by the standards of the time. He is said to have stood 6 ft 9 in tall and, despite his years, would have cut an imposing figure on any battlefield.

As for Maldon itself, it had been fortified by Edward the Elder in 916, with a view to protecting the North Sea approaches. Subsequent assaults by Danish raiding parties failed to reduce it, in part due to the support lent by Edward who was always ready to back up locally based resistance.

An audacious raiding party of Norwegians and Danes, in a total of ninety-three ships, set out in 991. One contingent of the raiders set their sights on Ipswich which they sacked before proceeding along the Essex coastline and putting in to the River Blackwater, to anchor at Northey Island, within easy striking distance of Maldon, though cut off from the mainland by a tidal river. There is some argument as to whether the raiders did, in fact, make for Heybridge, directly opposite Maldon, on the north bank of the River Chelmer. This is perhaps due to a misinterpretation of the Saxon word 'brycg', sometimes translated as 'bridge', with Heybridge being identified as the most likely place in the immediate neighbourhood to possess one. However, the term may also refer to a 'causeway', which would, in turn, lend support to the Northey Island location.

Learning of the swift movements of the raiders, Britnoth raised a force to combat the threat. The precise route of his march to Maldon is unknown, although it is reported that he sought hospitality at Ramsey Abbey, near Chatteris. The Abbot declined to accommodate anyone other than members of Britnoth's own household, a response which led to the alderman departing in a huff. The Abbot of Ely, on the other hand, who made an effort to cater for all Britnoth's followers, is said to have been given some of Britnoth's manors for his kindness.

By the time the Saxons arrived in the locality of Northey Island, the raiders were already in possession, their boats perhaps moored on the eastern edge and their main body of troops massed on the southern tip by the causeway that formed a tenuous link between the island and the mainland.

The Battle of Maldon

Virtually the only source for information about the Battle of Maldon is the famous but sadly incomplete poem of that name, which was probably written several years afterwards and, like many early poems describing battles, its main concern is with the exploits of individual combatants. Without it, however, the contest would be consigned to obscurity, existing only as another name in a long list of Saxon battles about which nothing is known.

The opening phase of the battle amounted to a war of words. The high tide made it impossible for the Danes to get over to the mainland. This gave Britnoth time to deploy his men – some of whom were mounted – to their best advantage, while the Danes could only stand and watch. They shouted across the water to Britnoth promising to depart in return for tribute. Not

The causeway linking Northey Island with the mainland, photographed from Northey Island at low tide.

surprisingly, Britnorth spurned the offer, past experience having shown that the Danes would probably proceed with their intended raid regardless.

As the tide ebbed, and the spear rattling approached a crescendo, the Saxons appointed three men to guard the causeway. And here the confrontation might have ended had not Britnoth agreed to the Danes' entreaties to be permitted to cross unmolested, so that a fair fight could ensue. The Saxons formed up behind a shield-wall against which pounded the spears and arrows of the invaders. The fighting was bitter, with brave men falling on both sides, but the shield-wall held firm.

For the Saxons, much depended upon Britnoth's stout-hearted, if somewhat over-chivalrous style of leadership. In the thick of combat, his advanced years began to tell as his younger, nimbler opponents outmanoeuvred him. Twice he was wounded and twice the offending missile was removed from his body. A third injury, a savage sword blow which may have all but severed an arm, rendered him helpless. Surrounded, he and his bodyguard were cut down. At this, one of his most trusted supporters, Godric, son of Odda, fled to the cover of woodland to the rear. Astride one of Britnoth's horses – a gift from the alderman – Godric was mistaken by many Saxons for Britnoth himself. Thinking that their leader had quitted the field, they too sought to save themselves, leaving only a small band of Britnoth's own retainers to fight on to the death.

The surviving fragment of the epic poem ends with descriptions of the heroic deaths of the faithful, who had promised to ride home with Britnoth in victory or else die with him on the field of battle. Exhausted and weakened by wounds, one by one they fell: Edward the tall, Etheric, a 'stalwart companion', Godric, son of Ethelgar, and many more. A tantalizing reference is made to Escferth, son of Ecglaf, described as a hostage from Northumbria, a skilful archer who continued to fight for as long as he was able to hold his bow. The battle may have ended in a defeat for the Saxons, but those who fought on sold their lives dearly. It is said that the Danes barely had enough survivors to man their ships.

Unable to pursue the Saxons who had fled, the Danes gave full vent to their fury against those who remained. Britnoth's head was cut off and carried away as a trophy but his torso was taken to Ely Abbey for burial. Uncovered in the north choir wall at Ely in 1772, it was found that, in preparing the remains for interment, the monks had replaced the head with a ball of wax.

In the days of Alfred, or even in those of Edward or Athelstan, perhaps Britnoth would not have been left to fight alone. Whatever Ethelred's instincts, he was counselled to make peace, and so the Danes received their hard-won tribute after all. It was a decision Ethelred would live to regret.

The Aftermath

It is sometimes claimed that the Saxon defeat at Maldon led to the introduction of Danegeld, the annual tax levied to buy peace from the Danes. In fact, such a tax had first been paid half a century earlier by Charles the Bald, King of the Franks. In 845 Ragnar the Viking had launched a daring raid on Paris. Having amassed an army strong enough to overwhelm the Danes, Charles foolishly divided it, enabling Ragnar to destroy it piecemeal before proceeding up the Seine to plunder the capital. His kingdom divided from within by bitter rivalries and open rebellion, Charles was unable to offer further resistance, and arranged to pay Ragnar the sum of 7,000 pounds of silver in return for a guarantee of six years' peace. The first such payment in England had occurred in 865, but it was only after the Battle of Maldon that the payments of the Danegeld proper began. Starting with 10,000 pounds of silver in 991, the sum demanded gradually increased, until in 1018 it had reached a colossal 72,000 pounds.

The initial 10,000 pounds of 991 may have represented part-payment of the greater sum of 22,000 pounds, mentioned in a treaty concluded between Ethelred and Olaf in that year. Within the terms of this treaty, the English agreed to guarantee the safety of foreign trading vessels in English estuaries, with the Danes likewise promising to respect English shipping overseas. Notwithstanding the additional stipulation that all past conflicts between the two countries should be forgotten – with the implication that friendly relations should continue into the foreseeable future – Olaf was back just three years later, in 994, in company with King Svein Forkbeard of Denmark, in an attempt to sack London. However, the siege proved unsuccessful, and Olaf and Svein were forced to retire, contenting themselves with indiscriminate raiding throughout Wessex and earning themselves, in addition to their plunder, Danegeld of 16,000 pounds. For good measure, Olaf took the scenic route home, via Wales and the Isle of Man, pillaging as he went.

The legends about Olaf and his deeds include one episode involving his conversion to Christianity, which appears to have occurred in 994 after the attack on London. In view of his subsequent behaviour, the process does not appear to have tempered his warlike disposition. Yet, he did promise once again that he would never return. This time, he kept his word, if only because he had set his sights on becoming King of Norway and, henceforth, would have little time to spare.

Olaf's preoccupation with weightier matters did nothing to ease the pressure on the Saxons, for there were many others ready and willing to take his place. The year 999 was particularly grievous, with Danish raiders penetrating the Medway as far as Rochester. Easily overcoming a weak force sent to meet them, they proceeded to ravage most of West Kent. Further depredations undertaken during the 1001–2 season led Ethelred to make a payment of 24,000 pounds in Danegeld.

Until 1002 the Duchy of Normandy had been used as a base by the Danes. Ethelred hoped to put a stop to this practice by marrying Duke Richard II of Normandy's sister, Emma. This deed accomplished, he ordered that all Danes in England on 13 November 1002 should be exterminated. One victim of this foolish edict was King Svein Forkbeard's sister, Gunnhild, whose death guaranteed Svein's future enmity. Particularly bloody raids followed in 1003–5 and again in 1009, after a short peace secured by a Danegeld payment of 36,000 pounds. The year 1009 ushered in several seasons of intensified assaults, at the end of which Svein Forkbeard would find himself King of England in all but name.

The Walk

Distance: 4 miles (6.44 km)

Begin in Promenade Park (Pathfinder 1123 862064) (Point A) bordering the River Blackwater. Walk alongside the river in an easterly direction towards the yacht club compound. To the left, between the compound and an unattractive household waste site, is a riverside path leading to Northey Island. Take this path and follow its course along the riverbank. Northey Island and the causeway can be seen in the middle distance.

As one approaches the island, an area of high ground comes into view on the right (Pathfinder 1123 861058). Although only a few metres above sea level, the existence of a topographical feature such as this could have proved of great value to the defending Saxons and could perhaps justify Britnoth's decision to invite the invaders over to the mainland.

Continue to the causeway (Pathfinder 1123 871058) (Point B) and walk across to the island. A strong voice easily carries across the decaying stillness of the landscape. Return to the mainland and take the gravel path leading to South House Farm, the site of which must have witnessed heavy fighting. Walk past the farm – the farmhouse is on the right, its outbuildings to the left – towards the line of bungalows and turn right into Mundon Road.

At the crossroads, turn left into Cross Road and then right into Fambridge Road. Another left turn into Granger Avenue, leading into Acacia Drive brings one out on Spital Road by the ruins of St Giles's

The Battle of Maldon, 991

N

River Blackwater

Northey Island

DANES

Causeway

B •

SAXONS

South House Farm

A •

Promenade Park

River Chelmer

The Hythe

St Mary's

Church St

Park Drive

D •

Mill Road

Mill Road

Mundon Road

Wantz Road

Cross Road

High Street

Market Hill

Friary

Chequers La

Silver St

Fambridge Road

All Saints

London Road

Granger Road

Washington Rd

Acacia Drive

Spital Road

St Peters Hospital

C •

St Giles's Hospital

By-Pass

1/2 Mile

Hospital (Pathfinder 1123 844065) (Point C), founded in 1164 as a refuge for citizens afflicted with leprosy. Turn towards the town centre and, en route, pause at St Peter's Hospital. A plaque on a wall in the grounds informs visitors that nearby – possibly just to the north, in London Road – is the site of the fortress established by Edward the Elder in 916.

Continue on to Silver Street and All Saints Church with its unique twelfth-century triangular tower and exterior statues, one of which depicts Britnoth standing in defiant attitude with shield and sword at the ready. At the end of Spital Road, on the right-hand side, is Chequers Lane which leads to the library, at the rear of which is the Friary, built on the site of an earlier Carmelite establishment, the order of the White Friars. Stones from the original house are said to be preserved in the walled garden.

Walk back to the High Street and down into Church Street. St Mary's Church (Pathfinder 1123 857058) (Point D) dates from 1130, although a church may well have stood here as early as the eighth century. A modern stained-glass window commemorates the Battle of Maldon.

At the end of Church Street is the four centuries old Jolly Sailor public house, overlooking the river, which is a suitable venue for refreshment. Return to the starting point via Hythe Quay, from where Thames sailing barges – some of which may still be seen – used to set off for London.

Something which should not be missed is the little-known 'Maldon Embroidery'. In 1991, as part of the millennium celebrations of the Battle of Maldon, it was decided to create a tapestry (along the lines of the Bayeux Tapestry) as a pictorial history of the town from Saxon times to the present. The second panel depicts the Battle of Maldon, including the death of

A panel from the Maldon Tapestry, depicting the Battle of Maldon. Note the Heinkel bomber which crashed near the site of the battle during the Second World War. The tapestry symbolizes a thousand years of warfare. (Maldon Millennium Trust)

Britnoth, whose body is shown being borne away for burial in Ely Cathedral. A somewhat incongruous element on this panel is a Second World War German bomber, which crashed near the battle site. At the time of writing (1995), the seven-panelled tapestry does not have a permanent home and the Tourist Information Office (see p 22) should be consulted for details of current display venues.

Further Explorations

On the western outskirts of Maldon is Beeleigh Abbey (Pathfinder 1123 840077), established by Robert Mantell during the reign of Henry II. This was the only Essex home of the little known Premonstratensian Order. In common with other minor houses, it was dissolved in 1536, but the calefactory, dormitory and chapter house have survived.

Throughout the English Civil War, Essex remained in Parliamentary hands and, as one might expect, boasts many Cromwellian connections. New Hall (Landranger 167 7509) near Boreham, is the surviving portion of a Tudor palace built by Henry VIII. Cromwell acquired it in 1651, but seems to have spent little time here, the house then passing to General Monck.

In the Holy Cross Church of Felstead (Landranger 167 6720) are the remains of Cromwell's first-born son, Robert. His youngest daughter, Frances, was married here in 1657 to Robert Rich, who died a few months later. It is said that a plan was conceived whereby Frances would wed the future Charles II, a marriage of convenience aimed at uniting the kingdom – but the plan came to nothing.

Ten miles to the east of Maldon is Bradwell on Sea (Landranger 168 0006), once a small fishing port. Beyond the village, on Sales Point, stood the Roman fort of Othona (Landranger 168 0308). About 500 ft square and with walls 12 ft thick, the structure was one of many Roman forts sited on the south and south-east coasts that grew in importance as a defence against Saxon raids. Only a fragment survives. By the seventh century AD, the fortress was already in a ruinous condition, but still sufficiently hospitable to give shelter to Cedd, a missionary priest from Lindisfarne, who built a chapel (St Peter on the Wall) on the foundations. Used as a barn in later centuries, it was reconsecrated in 1920; it is a place of pilgrimage to which, even today, few venture.

To the north east, at a distance of 16 miles, is Colchester (Landranger 168 0025), arguably the oldest town in England. Originally a large, fortified enclosure, covering a much greater acreage than the present day urban area, it first appears in recorded history under the name of Camulodunum, capital of the British King Cunobelin. It was also the first Roman town in Britain, and had the distinction of being destroyed by Boadicea. Two miles of the Roman wall erected to prevent a recurrence has been preserved (Pathfinder 1077 998255).

After the Saxons and the Danes came the Normans, and William the Conqueror gave the Crown properties and revenue of the town to Eudo, Seneschal of Normandy, who built the castle, whose imposing keep still stands (Pathfinder 1077 998253). Eudo also founded the Benedictine Abbey of St John, which quickly became one of the richest houses in Essex. Razed to the ground during the Reformation, only the gateway within the abbey gardens (Pathfinder 1077 99248) remains.

In 1216, during the baronial wars, the castle was the focus of a three-month siege – an affair which was overshadowed by a much later siege: that of the English Civil War. Staunchly Parliamentarian, the people of Colchester had donated £30,000 to the Parliamentarian cause, and one can imagine their concern when a 4,000-strong Royalist army, under the joint command of the Earl of Norwich, Sir George Lisle and Sir Charles Lucas, forced its way into the town on the afternoon of 12 June 1648. A Roundhead force commanded by Fairfax failed in an attempt to storm the defences, but cut off communications and settled down to starve the Royalists into submission. There had been little opportunity for the townsfolk to lay in provisions, and they were soon reduced to a wretched state. Many women who tried to leave were stripped and sent back. After seventy-six days, on 28 August, when it became clear that there was no hope of relief, the Royalist garrison surrendered. The Earl of Norwich was sent to Windsor for trial, but Lucas and Lisle were shot. Fairfax later explained that as both had been captured once before, they had broken the terms of their parole. As usual, the citizens of Colchester were the greatest sufferers. Some had starved to death. Much property had been destroyed and, notwithstanding the Parliamentarian leanings of the town, a heavy fine was imposed.

No trace of the Parliamentarian siege works remain. However, a portion of St Botolph's Priory (Pathfinder 1077 000250), almost destroyed by cannon fire, may still be seen, as can the Siege House in East Street (Pathfinder 1077 008254), pock-marked by musket balls. Before their execution, Lucas and Lisle were held in the yard of the Red Lion, in the High Street (Pathfinder 1077 995253). A monument marks the spot in Castle Park where they were shot (Pathfinder 1077 998255) and where it was once said that no grass would grow thereafter. They were laid to rest in St Giles's Church in the Lucas family vault.

Further Information

Tucked away to the rear of Chelmsford, Maldon is not easily approached by road. According to the map, the A414 via Chelmsford is the most direct route, but, with signposts at a premium, Chelmsford can be extraordinarily difficult to negotiate. An easier route is via the Hatfield Peverel turn-off on the Chelmsford–Colchester stretch of the A12. In Maldon itself, Promenade Park, the starting point for the walk, provides the best car parking facility.

Until 1964 Maldon had its own passenger railway line. Its station, said to be one of the finest examples of railway architecture in the country, has survived (Pathfinder 1123 854068). The Maldon by-pass runs along a portion of the old track. Today, the most convenient railway access is via Chelmsford. For details of rail services from London (Liverpool Street), telephone 0171 928 5100. A thirty-five minute Eastern National bus ride completes the journey; telephone 0345 000333 for details. There is no National Express coach service to Maldon. However, passengers on the London (Victoria) to Great Yarmouth route may alight at Chelmsford for the local bus connection. Visitors will find the Tourist Information Centre in Coach Lane (Pathfinder 1123 848071) very helpful; telephone 01621 851898).

Suggested background reading begins with the poem 'The Battle of Maldon'. An accessible version may be found in *The Oxford Book of War Poetry*, edited by Jon Stallworthy (OUP, 1984). This may be supplemented with accounts in Burne's *More Battlefields of England* and Smurthwaite's *Battlefields of Britain*. On the whole, however, Maldon is a battle many quite comprehensive studies have tended to ignore. Ordnance Survey maps for the area are Landranger 168 and Pathfinder 1123.

Strictly speaking, one should ask for permission to visit Northey Island, even though one's attention may be confined to the causeway. The island is primarily of importance to overwintering birds which suggests that summer is the most convenient season to visit. To make arrangements with the Warden (who will also provide details of the annual Open Day and, most important, times of high and low tides), telephone 01621 853142.

3
THE BATTLE OF HASTINGS
14 October 1066

Introduction

The Normans were a race of conquistadors with an empire which, at its height, included territory stretching from Wales to Syria but which by the year 1200 had all but disappeared. By the mid-tenth century Normandy was recognized as a state with boundaries and an established internal administration. In common with Britain, it had suffered from Danish incursions, resulting in Danish settlement and a measure of integration. It was a Dane, Rollo, who had founded Normandy in 911 from territory ceded to him by Charles the Simple, King of the Franks.

William – the Conqueror to be – was born in 1027 or 1028, the illegitimate son of Robert, Count of Heimois, who became Duke of Normandy by poisoning his elder brother. Robert's death in 1035, during a pilgrimage to the Holy Land, plunged Normandy into a civil war which the infant William, who had been named as heir to the Duchy, was fortunate to survive. But survive he did, attaining his majority and establishing his right to rule by force of arms at the Battle of Val-es-Dunes in 1047. Shortly after this famous victory, he was advised to marry, primarily to provide an heir. Through his bride Matilda, the daughter of the Count of Flanders, William developed an exceedingly tenuous claim to the throne of England, based on his kinship to Edward the Confessor, via Emma of Normandy, wife of Ethelred the Unready.

Meanwhile, in England, the Godwin family was busy consolidating its position as the power behind the throne of Edward the Confessor. Edward's mother, Emma, had been instrumental in introducing many Normans into the English court and, having been nurtured in Norman customs, Edward continued to curry favour with Normandy throughout his life. At some point in the early 1050s, it is said that he went so far as to name William as his heir, later sending Harold, son of Earl Godwin, to Normandy to confirm his decision. It was during this excursion that one of the most celebrated incidents connected with William's claim occurred.

Caught in a heavy storm, Harold was forced off course and into the hostile hands of Count Guy of Ponthieu, noted for his harsh treatment of victims of shipwrecks. However, through William's timely intervention, Harold was spared, ultimately finding himself in the Normandy capital of Rouen as William's guest. Lavishly entertained, Harold freely swore to uphold the latter's right to accede to the English throne upon Edward's death. The English version of the story depicts Harold being blown on to the coast of Ponthieu during a fishing expedition, with William tricking him into making the oath of fealty on a hidden chest of holy relics. Whatever the reason for Harold's overseas trip, at no time did he appear to be unduly worried about breaking his oath and clearly did not consider it binding.

When Edward died early in 1066 Harold seized the throne for himself. Duke William immediately set about drumming up support to obtain by force what he felt was his by right. The Papacy, keen to assume the role of arbiter in the matter, gave him its support. The Norman barons were rather more lukewarm in their appreciation of his plans, but were at length won over by the promise of extensive grants of land. Similarly, mercenaries from Brittany, Maine, Aquitaine and Anjou, seduced by the opportunities for pillage, flocked to his banner. A notable lack of enthusiasm was shown by King Philip of France who was warned of William's seemingly limitless ambitions.

Harold made haste to secure his realm, with the support of his standing army of housecarls and a navy which was already the envy of northern Europe. In July, while the fleet patrolled the Channel, Harold mobilized his troops on the Isle of Wight, to await the expected assault. But the north wind which was to restrict William to St Valery at the mouth of the Somme, also blew ill for Harold, who, after two months' fruitless waiting, had to disband his army when provisions ran short, and disperse his fleet for repairs. Harold himself retreated as far as London to await developments.

The Road to Hastings

William had already decided upon Pevensey as a suitable landing point for his invasion force. Remote enough to give him time to disembark his men, horses and stores, it was still close enough to Hastings to enable him to mount an attack on the significant seaport which he knew he must capture. All he needed now was a favourable wind, but still, week after week, it continued to blow down from the north. Becoming impatient, his great army remained intact only through the promise of the riches to be gained through looting. William himself would have grown even more restive, had he known that while he was stranded, Harold was marching north to meet the challenge of another invasion, thus leaving the south coast undefended. In desperation, William turned to his holy relics. The remains of St Edmund, brought forth from the Church of St Valery, were paraded along the seashore. The very next day – 27 September 1066 – the wind changed.*

It must be remembered that this was no mere seasonal raiding party of the kind the Danes had mounted in recent centuries, but a vast undertaking aimed at the permanent conquest of an emergent nation. Soldiers, armour, weapons, supplies – all had to be organized on what was, for the time, a vast scale. The fleet itself may have numbered as many as 700 vessels, including many specially constructed troop-carriers. The Bayeux Tapestry depicts open-decked, single-masted vessels similar in design to the Danish long-ships. Under William's personal supervision, his men worked all day so that all might be ready to set sail that very evening.

William's own flagship, the *Mora*, led the armada on the great adventure and soon outpaced the rest of the fleet, so that as morning broke, he found himself alone and had to wait for everyone else to catch up. The chroniclers would have us believe that, regardless of the perilous nature of the journey in what was a comparatively primitive craft, he breakfasted comfortably – even luxuriously – until the heavily laden boats struggled into sight, after which they pressed on to Pevensey, which they reached at around 9 a.m. on 28 September.

William was first ashore, stumbling as he set foot on Anglo-Saxon soil. Shrugging off what could be seen as a bad omen, he picked himself up, announcing that he had already taken the English earth in his hands. A body of armed fighting men followed, but they met with no resistance. Clearly, despite the fact that the wind had changed, they were not expected, and so a beach-head could be established without undue difficulty.

The question of how William transported and disembarked up to 3,000 horses is one that has long puzzled historians. The Normans may have waited for the tide to ebb, leading the horses out on to dry land, or they may have hauled them off. The remaining option would have involved some design modifications, to allow for a ship's sides to be drawn up and down, like a drawbridge, or for the provision of some sort of gangway within, by which the horses could be led to and from the bottom of the boats. However it was achieved, the end result was a successful one, and by midday the army

---

* William was also quite capable of summoning help from other quarters. In 1071, for example, he summoned a witch 'to disconcert by her magic all the warlike devices of the Saxons'.

was making camp in Pevensey's Roman fort (see p 35), their advance party having already slaughtered the town's inhabitants. Word must somehow have reached Hastings too, for when the Normans approached on 29 September, the town offered no resistance, and William now commanded a safe harbour for his fleet and a good road to London.

News of the Norman landing reached Harold at York, where he was celebrating his victory at the Battle of Stamford Bridge, which had been fought on 25 September. Always the man of action, the king wasted no time musing on the turn of events which had drawn him away from the south coast. On 2 October he began the long march south, accompanied by those of his housecarls who were still battle-worthy, and collecting new recruits along the way. Three days later he reached London and, somewhat late in the day, sent his fleet to patrol the Channel. During his stay in the capital, Harold made a pilgrimage to Waltham, where he hoped to acquire divine approval for his cause from the abbey's famous relic, the Holy Rood. According to contemporary accounts, the Rood bowed to the king. Although interpreted by the monks as a sign that he was about to be deposed, a favourable result in the battle to come could just as easily have led to an appropriate reassessment.

There now occurred an exchange of messages between the king and the prospective conqueror, with William accusing Harold of breaking his oath and Harold replying that he only swore it in the first instance to gain his freedom. Both leaders were counselled by followers who gave both good and bad advice. William had been advised to march on London, which he had refused to do, contenting himself by laying waste the surrounding countryside. Meanwhile, attempts were made to dissuade Harold from seeking a decisive conflict at a time when he and most of his seasoned troops were still battle-weary.

Fortunately for William and unhappily for Harold, neither took the advice he was offered, and on 12 October Harold left London with all the men he could muster, appointing as a meeting-place for those to follow a well known landmark on the South Downs, 'The Place of the Hoar Apple Tree', on Caldbec Hill.

The Battle of Hastings

On 13 October 1066, Harold reached Caldbec Hill, his troops staggering wearily into camp after their 60 mile march. It is said that men were still arriving the following day – after the battle had started. According to the victors, the evening of the 13 October was spent by the Saxons in carousal and by the Normans in prayer.

The Normans, fearing a surprise night attack, remained on the alert throughout the night. At dawn they advanced as far as Telham Hill. Harold, they discovered, had also advanced – to Battle Hill, an extremely advantageous position comprising a ridge of high ground (a site now occupied by Battle Abbey). At this point, William fell victim to another unfortunate omen when his servants put on his chainmail back to front. Once again, he had the wit to turn a potentially damaging situation to his advantage by arguing that this merely signified his change from a duke to a king, and thus allaying the fears of his superstitious followers.

Of William's 8,000 or so men, perhaps 3,000 were mounted knights and men at arms; the remainder were lightly armed foot soldiers, including a complement of archers. They were drawn up in three divisions, a pattern of deployment which would become standard practice on British battlefields for centuries. In the centre, William commanded his Normans. On his right was the Franco-Flemish contingent led by Roger de Montgomery, and to his left, soldiers from Brittany under Count Alan Fergeant.

The Saxon army which, as already noted, may have been incomplete, could not have been much larger than the invading force, and was massed behind a single shield-wall up to 1,000 yards in length. Each side must have been an awesome sight for the other to behold as the mounted Normans moved down Telham Hill to assume their battle positions some 500 yards from a seemingly impenetrable wall of Saxon shields.

The Normans made the first move, with their archers running forward to test the efficacy of the shield-wall. Their arrows did little damage and the shield-wall held firm. William then ordered his spear-men to the attack. Struggling up the hill, they were met with a barrage of assorted missiles, and although they pressed on to the shield-wall itself, they were unable to make any lasting impression upon it. Neither did the Norman cavalry that now lumbered forward meet with any more success, men and horses being cut down by fiercely wielded axes. On the left of the line, it was all too much for the Bretons, who were forced to retreat, closely pursued by some Saxons who broke ranks. At this stage, according to tradition, William removed his helmet, so that all might see him, and led his cavalry on a counter-charge into the midst of the Saxons who had left the safety of their hill-top position.

There now occurred one of the curious pauses, lasting perhaps one hour, that are recognized as a not uncommon feature of medieval British battles. In such strength-sapping toe-to-toe bludgeoning contests, even the hardiest professional soldier needed some respite and so, as if by unspoken agreement between the protagonists, hostilities were suspended; this allowed the Saxons to repair their shield-wall and the Normans to regroup.

The manoeuvres which led to the climax of the battle are unclear. According to some authorities, the fighting developed into a series of Norman charges which, as the shadows of the October day lengthened, gradually wore down the Saxons, who began to slip away, until William's cavalry was able to penetrate the depleted ranks. However, the number of assaults, launched uphill and over heavy ground, of which the invading army was capable must have been limited. At some stage, William probably opted for a single all-or-nothing effort to turn the tide of battle in his favour.

Appreciative of the fact that the Saxons could be drawn from their impregnable position to pursue retreating cavalry, it is likely that the duke ordered the Bretons forward one last time, with instructions to feign a retreat, so that his own cavalry could make a concerted effort to force its way through the resultant gaps in the shield-wall. The ruse worked. As the Saxons leapt forward to harass the Bretons, William's cavalry rushed in – the pressure of the Norman horsemen transforming the shield-wall from a straight line into a semi-circular formation. At the same time, the Norman archers changed tactics. Instead of firing directly at the Saxon shields, they raised their aim so that their arrows rained down from above.

As the Norman cavalry pressed home their advantage, an arrow struck Harold in the eye. At this point, more of his men began to slip away, although the faithful fought on. The shield-wall rapidly diminished until it deteriorated into a circle of Harold's bodyguards surrounding their dying king. One by one they fell until, unprotected, Harold himself was hacked to death. According to contemporary chroniclers, the fleeing Saxons were

Detail from the Bayeux Tapestry. Some doubt has been cast on the story that Harold was killed when struck in the eye by an arrow. However, if the action as recorded by the tapestry is accepted as authentic, then the figure depicted grasping the arrow below the name Harold must go some way towards settling the argument in favour of the traditional explanation.

pursued by tired horsemen, many of whom met their deaths by charging recklessly into a deep ravine known as Malfosse.

With the benefit of hindsight, it is easy to criticize Harold's strategy; he would have been better advised to defend the Sussex shore; he should have capitalized on his advantages early in the battle; his energies should have been directed towards ensuring that the Saxon shield-wall remained firm. In the final analysis, it would have been expecting too much of any monarch to combat two invasions – within three weeks of one another – at opposite ends of his realm. It speaks much for Harold's abilities as a leader of men that he came within a whisker of achieving the elusive double victory.

The Aftermath

The new King of England spent some time examining the battlefield, while his men stripped the dead and dispatched the dying. William ordered his own tent to be set up amid the carnage where, deaf to the entreaties of his bodyguard, he spent the night. It was not until the following day that the extent of the slaughter could be assessed. In the famous 'Roll of the Conqueror's Companions', lost in the fourteenth century, William recorded the names of those of his noblemen who had fallen. And although he permitted the relatives of the English dead to remove their remains for burial, most of the corpses were left to rot. Their blanched bones, picked clean by the wolves which freely roamed the land, could still be seen strewn across the ridge they had so heroically defended, seventy years later.

William was especially anxious to locate Harold's mutilated body and, for this purpose, summoned both Harold's mother, Gytha, and his mistress, Edith Swan-Neck. When Edith had identified her lover, for whom she had borne three sons, by certain tattoo marks, his remains were buried by the sea – some said as a mark of honour for a man who had striven so courageously to defend his native shore, although others saw it as an act of mockery aimed at one who had tried and failed.

At some stage, probably after the Conqueror's death, Harold's remains were removed to Waltham Abbey for interment, but even this did not restrict the growth of a legend to the effect that he had survived the Battle of Hastings. Nursed back to health, so the story goes, he spent the rest of his life travelling on the Continent in an effort to secure support for plans to regain his crown.

As far as hard facts are concerned, William's victory at Hastings by no means guaranteed his acceptance by the Anglo-Saxons. Both victor and vanquished were cautious. The two northern earls, Edwin and Morcar, conferred with the archbishops of Canterbury and of York but, disappointed by the choice of a successor to Harold – the ten-year-old Edgar the Atheling – they withdrew to the north.

William spent almost a week in Hastings, apparently waiting for the defeated people to come to pay homage. In fact, he was making plans for securing his base of operations, which he achieved by sending to Normandy for reinforcements – in plentiful supply as a result of his success – and by seizing the major ports on the south-east coast. While guaranteeing clemency to those who threw themselves on his mercy, such as the garrison of Dover Castle, he was quick to punish any who defied him, butchering the citizens of Romney who had attacked a group of Norman knights.

The ultimate objective was London. Instead of marching directly on the capital, William embarked on a wide sweep to the south, laying waste all the land en route. Unable to effect an entry via London Bridge, he continued along the south bank of the Thames to Wallingford, where he met with the Archbishop of Canterbury, whose task it was to pave the way for what was to be the official surrender. This event occurred at Berkhamsted on 21 December 1066, when Edwin and Morcar, accompanied by Edgar the Atheling, formally asked William to accept the English Crown. In a response very similar to that of Richard, Duke of Gloucester, almost four hundred years later, William thought it seemly to hesitate, allowing himself the luxury of accepting by the persuasion of his enemies what he had, in fact, taken by force.

Finally, on 25 December 1066, the Conqueror was crowned King William I of England, in a ceremony which emphasized his hereditary rights, as opposed to the right of conquest. For the second time within a year, the English magnates gathered in Westminster Abbey to acclaim a new monarch. On this occasion, however, when the customary question 'Will you have this prince to be your king?' was put to those present, the voices of those responding with 'Yea' were drowned by the enthusiastic rival cries of 'Oui'.

The Walk

Distance: 3½ miles (5.63 kms)

Begin at Battle Abbey car park (Pathfinder 1290 749157) (Point A). Leaving the car park, turn sharp left to follow the line of the high wall. The wide bridleway hugs the wood known as 'Long Plantation' to the left. Occasionally, where trees overhang the path, horses have rendered the path

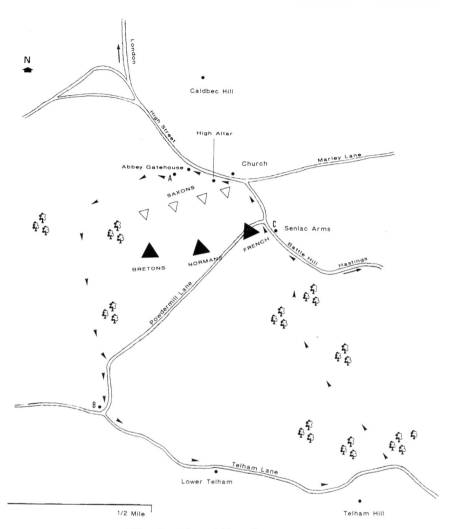

The Battle of Hastings, 1066

very muddy. The trees also obscure one's view of Battle Hill, the slopes of which can be glimpsed through gaps in the undergrowth which thins out as one progresses. At the end of the wood, the path branches out to left and right. Follow the path round to the left and continue walking south to Powdermill Lane (the B2095). Ignoring the scrap-yard on the left, turn into the field to the right and follow the wide grassy track which runs downhill

Battle Abbey from the junction of the B2095 and Telham Lane. Battlefield exploration involves far more than an examination of the often limited geographical area of a battle's climax!

parallel with the road to the junction of Telham Lane (Pathfinder 1290 744144) (Point B).

Cross the road (with care) and walk up Telham Lane. Quite a steep climb to begin with, the route levels out into a more leisurely ascent to Telham Hill. A walkable grass verge develops as one progresses although it is necessary, at intervals, to move over from right to left so as to avoid oncoming traffic on 'blind' corners. At Lower Telham – an isolated cottage – (Pathfinder 1290 751141) a gap in the hedge on the left provides a splendid view of the abbey and Battle Hill, along the crest of which the Saxons formed their shield-wall. Continue walking over the railway line to a footpath (Pathfinder 1290 760141) branching off to the left in front of Telham Hill.

Before following the footpath down through the field, pause and take stock of the topography. Telham Hill, over one's right shoulder, would have provided William with an excellent observation post, although it is over a mile away from the Saxon lines; this fact may throw doubt on claims that he retired to the hill at intervals throughout the battle. The Bretons would have advanced to the left, beyond the railway line, with the Flemish contingent to the right, and William's Norman troops in the centre – along one's own line of advance towards the trees.

The path through Malthouse Wood can be found by skirting the trees to the left. Walk through the neck of wood and emerge into the rolling, open landscape on the other side. Ahead is more woodland to the south of Telham Court School. The path here is narrow and inclined to be overgrown during the summer months. A little disappointingly, it remains enclosed until its conclusion on Battle Hill. Open ground to the left, along the Flemish line of march, is now a venue for car-boot sales.

Turn left into Battle Hill and cross over the railway line. At this point, it is appropriate to seek refreshment at the Senlac Arms (Point C). Continue to follow the main road round to the junction with Marley Lane. From this point, a good view of Caldbec Hill may be obtained. Walk on past St Mary's Church into Upper Lake and back to the abbey.

No exploration of the area would be complete without a visit to English Heritage's abbey grounds (adding an extra mile or so to the overall distance). Visitors are guided around the centre of the battlefield by a series of recordings accessed by handsets – a somewhat complicated system lacking in visual impact. The remains of the abbey itself, founded in 1070 by William in atonement for the bloodshed four years' earlier, are well worth visiting. The site of the high altar, on the very spot where Harold fell, may be viewed, along with lovingly restored ruins of later additions to the complex.

Further Explorations

It is not unreasonable to suggest that any projected further exploration of the area should begin with Hastings. Despite lending its name to the most celebrated battle in English history, Hastings has seen very little military action except a series of successful French raids during the course of the Hundred Years War. As one of the Cinque Ports which assumed a leading role in the defence of the nation, its vulnerability to these frontal assaults is perhaps surprising. Of Hastings Castle (Landranger 199 8209), built between 1068 and 1080 by Robert, Count of Eu, little now remains. In 1216 it was slighted by King John, who feared that its possible capture by the French might lead to its use as a base for an army of invasion. Rebuilt by Henry III, it fell victim to coastal erosion so that by the sixteenth century, it was already a ruin.

Altogether a more traditionally romantic castle is to be found to the south west of Battle, at Herstmonceux (Landranger 199 6410). Built by Sir Roger de Fiennes (later the first Lord Dacre) between 1440 and 1447 on a site commanding the Pevensey levels, it was modelled rather more on continental than on British castles. A red-brick structure with dimensions of 219 ft by 208 ft, the castle – like many others of its day – comprised a virtually self-sufficient community, with a bakehouse, brewhouse, distillery and a wealth of private apartments. A spacious and luxurious private dwelling, its defences were also formidable, with a moat and a drawbridge – operating on the counter-balance principle – flanked by two towers, the watch tower and the signal tower, containing rows of arrow-loops with oiletts for firearms. Herstmonceux, like all good castles, has a ghost: a phantom drummer, a terrible figure standing 9 ft high, reputed to have been a soldier killed at Agincourt.

The Church of All Saints, adjacent to Herstmonceux Castle, contains the fifteenth-century Dacre Chapel, commemorating several generations of the famous family of warriors, members of which were present at both Towton in 1461 and at Flodden in 1513.

Although Hastings and Herstmonceux castles receive little or no mention in the standard castle guidebooks, the same cannot be said of Pevensey Castle (Landranger 199 6404), which lies 13 miles to the west of Hastings, on the A259. Part of the attraction of Pevensey lies in the fact that a Norman castle was built within a Roman fort. Known in Roman times as Anderida, it was the main garrison post in Sussex. The surviving walls, over 10 ft thick, enclose an area of between 9 and 10 acres. Built during the eleventh century at the east end of the fort, the Norman castle comprised a rectangular keep (the Roman wall forming one side), with a bailey extending into the fort, the gatehouse and wall towers being added in the thirteenth century.

Following the Roman withdrawal, Anderida was pillaged by the Saxons. The Danes carried out a number of bloody raids, and later sieges were undertaken by William Rufus (whose ghostly army is still sometimes seen marching on the castle) in 1088, by King Stephen in 1144, by Simon de Montfort in 1265 and by Yorkists in 1399 when the Pelhams defended it for the Lancastrians.

Pevensey, once a member of the influential Confederation of Cinque Ports, has long since been left high and dry, separated from the sea by the sandy dunes of the 'Crumbles' – its desolate coastline now guarded only by a line of decaying Martello towers (see p 48).

Further Information

Battle lies on the A2100, off the A21 London–Hastings road. The A21 can be joined at Junction 5 of the M25 and is 'duelled' as far as Tunbridge Wells so a motor journey, if undertaken at off-peak periods, is not too onerous. Car parking is available in the Battle Abbey car park or off the High Street in front of the Gate House. A National Express coach service operates from London (Victoria); telephone 0990 808080 for details. Remarkably, Battle still has its own railway station, on the London (Charing Cross)–Hastings line and for details of rail services, telephone 0171 928 5100. In all, Battle is one of the most accessible battlefields.

Reading material is prolific. All the major battlefield texts carry chapters. Solid accounts will be found in Young and Adair's *From Hastings to Culloden*; Seymour's *Battles in Britain: 1066–1547*; and Burne's *Battlefields of England*. Of the more detailed accounts, two of the most readable are Piers Compton's *Harold the King* and Rupert Furneaux's *Conquest 1066*. Christopher Gravett's *Hastings 1066: The Fall of Saxon England* in Osprey's excellent Campaign series is indispensable. An excellent illustrated booklet, *1066 Origin of a Nation* by Michael Phillips, is available in the English Heritage bookshop. In addition, on site purchase of Plantagenet Somerset Fry's official English Heritage guide book, *The Battle of Hastings and the Story of Battle Abbey*, is essential to the Visitor Centre tour. Ordnance Survey maps of the area are Landranger 199 and Pathfinder 1290. The Tourist Information Centre, open daily (including Sundays) is opposite Battle Abbey in the High Street (telephone 01424 773721).

English Heritage has endeavoured to provide first-class facilities for tourists. Clearly, on-going restoration of the abbey is an expensive business and the (1995) site entrance fee of £3.00 per adult is put to good use. For details of Visitor Centre opening times and current entrance fees, telephone 01424 773792.

4
THE BATTLE OF LEWES
14 May 1264

Introduction

Henry III was crowned at Gloucester on 28 October 1216 shortly after the death of his father, King John. He was nine years of age, and destined to reign until his death fifty-six years later. Much of this time was taken up with futile – some would say pathetic – attempts to establish himself as a force to be reckoned with on the European stage. For example, he tried to establish his youngest son, Edmund Crouchback, as King of Sicily, promising to provide the sum of £90,000 to prosecute a war against rival candidates. The Great Council refused to grant the necessary funds and the idea was abandoned. A second more successful but similarly expensive project involved the election in 1257 of Richard of Cornwall, Henry's brother, as ruler of Germany, with the grand title 'King of the Romans', a somewhat meaningless office given the fragmented nature of the German empire at the time, coupled with the fact that, following his appointment, Richard continued to live in Isleworth.

Another country comprising a conglomeration of petty principalities was Wales. Henry had used existing divisions in the north to extend English influence but by 1254 the Welsh were enjoying a measure of unaccustomed unity under Llewelyn II of Gwynedd. Two years later, a war of liberation drove all English sympathizers from Welsh lands, a state of affairs which an abortive English campaign did nothing to reverse. The baronage was furious at these latest antics of a king whom they had come to regard as an incompetent wastrel and at a Great Council meeting in April 1258 Henry was presented with an ultimatum within the terms of which he would effectively transfer his power to an assembly of barons committed to reform.

One of the most outspokenly critical of the barons was the king's own brother-in-law, Simon de Montfort, who had arrived in England in 1229 from his home in the Ile-de-France to claim his inheritance – the earldom of

Leicester. Initial friendship between the two men, engendered by Simon's marriage to Henry's sister, eventually deteriorated, certainly on Henry's side, into barely disguised enmity and Simon quickly emerged as the leader of the opposition.

The barons' demands were embodied in the 1258 Provisions of Oxford which allowed for a council of fifteen members, to be elected by both the Royal party and the baronage, which would be responsible for government, with the support of a Parliament of twelve barons meeting three times a year. Although some lip service was paid to the rights of the third-estate, the scheme really amounted to a transfer of absolute power from monarchy to baronage. This did not go unnoticed by the shire knights whom, as tenants of the barons, feared the excesses of a more powerful baronage. When the king held court at Westminster in the autumn of 1259, a deputation of knights proposed measures of their own, and the barons considered it expedient to modify their plans accordingly even though their power over their tenants was limited in the process. The knights were supported in their demands by the king's elder son, Prince Edward, who had hoped to prevail by fomenting divisions.

Confident at least of Papal support, Henry responded to these outbreaks of democratic fervour by proclaiming that he alone had the right to appoint his ministers. Against this display of defiance the barons backed down and acquiesced to a review of the Provisions of Oxford, which were developed into the Provisions of Westminster. Disgusted at this turn of events, Simon went back to France for some months, returning in the spring of 1263 to take charge of the situation by leading a rebel baronial army through the Welsh Marches to challenge all who opposed the Provisions. In the early stages of his crusade, Simon even enjoyed the backing of Richard of Cornwall, while the king and queen, in company with Prince Edward, locked themselves up in the Tower of London. Queen Eleanor tried to escape to Windsor via the Thames but, attacked by the rioting populace, she was forced to take refuge with the Bishop of London.

Nevertheless, fortune's pendulum continued to swing, for although on 21 July 1263 Henry agreed to observe the Provisions – and, further, to hand over all castles to baronial control – by the autumn, the Royal party was again gaining support, and Simon was compelled to agree to refer the whole question to Louis IX of France for arbitration.

Few can have doubted the outcome when, on 24 January 1264, Louis gave judgement in what would become known as the Mise of Amiens. In the presence of Henry, the French monarch dismissed the Provisions, confirming the principle of the Divine Right of a King to choose his own advisors – the only saving grace being that Simon had satisfied himself by sending representatives to Amiens, while he remained in readiness in England. . . .

The Road to Lewes

Louis' decision at Amiens proved to be the spark which ignited the long-smouldering fire and plunged England into civil war. Throughout the crisis, confrontation in the Marches between Simon and Roger Mortimer had never been far away, and immediately after Amiens, trouble flared up again. A rebel army under the command of Simon's son, Henry, was dispatched to the west to deal with it, and succeeded in capturing Radnor Castle. In retaliation (for the conflict was very retaliatory in nature) Prince Edward seized, and handed over to Mortimer, the castles of one of the Earl of Leicester's supporters, Humphrey de Bohun.

On the road home from the Marches, the de Montforts managed, by stealth, to gain entry to Gloucester, but were unable to make much headway in taking Gloucester Castle which had been fortified by Prince Edward. Realizing that his force was heavily outnumbered, Edward reached an agreement with his besiegers to the effect that he would encourage King Henry to come to heel. However, as soon as the rebel army had withdrawn, the prince imprisoned all who had supported the baronial cause, and marched to join his father who had returned from France and established his headquarters at Oxford, with the support of his brother, Richard of Cornwall.

There followed further negotiations for peace. Arrangements were made for talks to take place at Brackley in Northamptonshire but, instead, the time allowed to organize the parley was used by both sides to prepare for war. Simon himself, confined to Kenilworth with a broken leg sustained in a riding accident, and in no mood for a peaceful settlement, was annoyed at the way his eldest son had been duped by Prince Edward. Cheered to some extent by rioting taking place in London, he decided to remove to the capital, where he was joined by Gilbert de Clare.

The king used the lull to gather a substantial army which included foreign mercenaries and Scots – a ploy which was generally counter-productive in that it tended to incense any Englishmen who were undecided as to which party they would support – and marched on Northampton, which was held by the rebel barons under the direction of Peter de Montfort and Simon the younger. Although defended most vigorously, the town fell through the treachery of the Prior of St Andrews who admitted the Royalists through a breach in the priory walls. Simon the younger was taken prisoner and the Royal mercenaries reaped their reward by indulging in an orgy of barbarities.

Simon the elder, having heard of the attack on Northampton, had marched north in an attempt to lift the short-lived siege. At St Albans, having either learned of the collapse of the garrison, or else suspecting a rebellion in his absence, he returned to London. In any event, there followed a general massacre of the capital's Jews, an event for which little justification was usually required, and which went some way towards replenishing rebel coffers.

There now followed a curious interlude in which, apparently intent on avoiding a head-on confrontation, the king and his supporters concentrated their attention on the Midland counties, while the rebels attempted to subjugate the south. The Royalists lost no time in laying waste Derbyshire and Staffordshire, and securing Leicester and Nottingham. On the other hand, Simon spent much time and effort in trying to take Rochester. With the aid of the latest siege-engines, the town was taken and pillaged, although the formidable castle held out. Prince Edward had hoped to capitalize on the rebel preoccupation with Rochester by marching on London but, by abandoning the siege, Simon managed to forestall him, racing back to the city's defence. In response, Edward executed a brilliant manoeuvre by crossing the Thames at Kingston and making for Rochester. The token rebel force which had remained at Rochester suffered a particularly cruel fate – on his arrival, the prince ordered that their hands and feet should be cut off.

By 1 May 1264, with the Royal army having moved on to capture Tonbridge Castle, belonging to the Earl of Gloucester, it may have seemed as if everything was going the king's way. In fact, the rebel barons continued to hold some strong cards. Not least of these were the Cinque Ports, held by rebel sympathizers. Royal attempts to persuade the Wardens to muster a fleet to sail up the Thames to attack London, the strongest rebel card of all, proved fruitless, and the king turned his attention to Lewes, arriving on 11 May at the head of an army now running dangerously short of provisions – one of the hazards of embarking upon a prolonged campaign with a large army at a comparatively early stage in the season.

Seeking to bring the issue to a head, Simon had left London on 6 May and, having located the Royal army, marched to Fletching, 9 miles to the north of Lewes, where his army, augmented by local archers, made camp within the Forest of Weald. On 12 May Simon sent emissaries to the king with one final offer to make peace. This was largely a matter of form, there being little hope that Henry would actually accede to the reiterated rebel demands that he must subscribe to the Provisions of Oxford. As expected, his response was one of defiance and so, on the evening of 13 May, the rebels prepared for battle.

The Battle of Lewes

In the early morning of 14 May 1264 the barons quitted their campsite. Morale was high, and it is said that a strong religious sentiment pervaded

The view from Lewes Castle, looking towards Offham Hill, where the rebel barons drew up their men.

the ranks – each rebel tunic, in true crusading spirit, bore a large white cross to both front and rear. Even so, the rebel army, about 5,000 strong, was outnumbered by 2 to 1 and, with only 600 cavalry, it was important for Simon to seek out an advantageous position. He found it on Offham Hill which overlooked Lewes from a height of some four hundred feet. On the broad plateau crowning the hill, Simon was able to deploy his troops with confidence, helped, no doubt, by intelligence gleaned from a solitary Royalist look-out who had fallen asleep at his post. Notwithstanding his numerical inferiority, Simon was still able to form three divisions and a reserve, the latter under his own charge. Command of the centre was entrusted to the young Earl of Gloucester, with Henry de Montfort on the right and Nicholas de Segrave and Henry de Hastings on the left.

Despite their poor scouting arrangements – a symptom of over-confidence – the Royalists must have been aware of Simon's movements on Offham Hill at a relatively early stage. King Henry and his brother, Richard, were billeted to the south of the town, in the vicinity of St Pancras Priory, and would have depended upon Prince Edward, lodged in the castle, for advance notice of activities on the high ground to the north.

Although the Royal army may have comprised over 9,000 men, and included 1,500 cavalry, its advantage over the rebels in this respect was dissipated by the fact that Edward's men took the field in advance of the king's force. Making their way steadily uphill, the prince's cavalry headed towards the rebel left wing upon which they launched a ferocious assault. De Segrave's front lines wilted and then gave way, his troops fleeing before the royal horsemen, who pursued them over the hill, down towards Offham and beyond. It developed into an increasingly unruly general pursuit, which is said to have gone on for a distance of 4 miles, with some rebels being pursued as far as Croydon.

Meanwhile, the remainder of the Royal army, with Henry in what would have been the centre had Edward held his ground, and Richard on the left, was now entering the fray. According to some secondary sources, Simon saw to it that the remaining rebels held their ground and allowed the royalists to struggle uphill before launching a counter-attack. Others argue that Simon, favouring the impetus of a downhill charge, decided to take the battle to the king. Whichever is correct, the fact remains that Edward's absence from the field was to prove decisive.

It would appear that each Royal column became preoccupied with its own survival and was unable to support the other. Richard's troops seem to have given way under pressure, much as de Segrave's men had done earlier, and they turned tail with Henry de Montfort's right wing in pursuit. The king's column met with more success, holding its ground until Simon threw in his reserve to overwhelm it in the vicinity of the modern gaol. The Earl of Gloucester may well have played a vital role in the centre and doubtless felt that his contribution to Simon's success merited greater recognition than he was given.

Loyal supporters covered King Henry's retreat to the priory as the rebels charged victoriously into Lewes. Cut off from his command and unable to reach the town, Richard was reduced to barricading himself inside a windmill, and by early afternoon, when Prince Edward returned to the battlefield, although sporadic fighting was still taking place, the Royalists had been well and truly beaten – many having been pursued into the marshes to the south of the priory where they sank beneath the weight of their armour. Bravely the prince fought his way through the ranks of his enemies in a forlorn attempt to revive the fighting spirit of the Royalist refugees inside the castle walls.

Total casualties have been calculated at around 3,000. This is perhaps one of the few instances in the annals of medieval warfare when such an estimate may be too conservative. Certainly, few of the leaders were killed, but casualties sustained by the Royalists must have been particularly high for, unlike de Segrave's rebels in the earlier part of the battle, they had no avenue of escape. However, some did escape into exile in France, while, through a process of mediation in which both Franciscan and Dominican friars figured prominently, the surrender of the king, Prince Edward and Richard of Cornwall was negotiated. Simon had won a famous victory.

The Aftermath

The peace negotiations between the warring factions resulted in the Mise of Lewes, an agreement which in some respects seemed to favour the vanquished rather more than the victor. Despite the discouraging views of Louis IX and Pope Urban IV, Simon was pinning his hopes on the Provisions of Westminster as offering the best all-round solution to the constitutional crisis. Thinking that Louis might have revised his opinion in the light of the rebel victory at Lewes, Simon decided to gamble on acquiring his support by including within the Mise of Lewes a clause allowing for arbitration by a panel of French bishops and nobles. In the event, Louis did not respond and Simon was left to proceed alone.

Accordingly, towards the end of June 1264, a new scheme entitled 'A Form for the Government of the King and Kingdom' was launched. Seemingly quite modest in its ambitions, it comprised a stipulation that in future, the King's Council – to be composed entirely of Englishmen – should be appointed by a board of three electors, and that its role would be to advise the king on the matter of his ministerial appointments. The three electors were to be Simon himself, Stephen Berksted, Bishop of Winchester,

The seal of Simon de Montfort. (Historical Association)

and the Earl of Gloucester. With more Montfortian supporters appointed to the Council, it could be seen that Simon's control over the king would be only marginally less than absolute.

Of equal concern to Simon was the consolidation of his victory in terms of strengthening his military position. In this respect, too, he appeared to be bent on establishing a dynasty of his own, with some of the strongest fortresses in the land being given over to the control of members of the de Montfort family. Doubtless he considered it essential to appoint people he could trust to key positions but, again, this was something his enemies could turn to their advantage.

It has sometimes been remarked that from Simon's victory at Lewes to his defeat and death in the Evesham campaign just over one year later, England was in a state of siege. Now in France Queen Eleanor redoubled her efforts to raise troops for an invasion and, throughout the summer of 1264, an English army, gathered in the king's name, kept a close watch on the Channel. The expected danger did not materialize because Eleanor ran out of money, but Simon, with problems enough to keep him occupied nearer home, could not relax his guard.

There remained particularly stubborn pockets of Royalist resistance; Simon was most concerned about those in the Welsh Marches, where Roger Mortimer and James Audley had to be brought to heel. In the realm at large, there was anarchy, with devastation and despair on a scale not known since the civil wars of Stephen's reign. Merchants were unable to conduct their business and even the peasantry was robbed of what little it possessed. Amid it all, Simon continued to concentrate on strengthening his own position, from the security of the newly fortified Kenilworth Castle.

Perhaps Simon was at his most powerful during Christmas 1264 when, seemingly oblivious to the hardships of those whom he appeared to regard as his subjects, he held court at Kenilworth, surrounded by his friends and supporters. But even before the feasting began, the seeds of his downfall had been sown, with an unseemly show of support by the Earl of Gloucester for his fellow Marcher lords, Mortimer and Audley. Although they had been banished, albeit temporarily, Gloucester offered them his protection, allowing them to remain in the Marches. When called to account for his behaviour, he refused (wisely) to appear before Simon. Instead, he gave vent to his feelings of resentment at being excluded from the process of government by accusing the Earl of Leicester of appropriating to himself and his rapacious sons all the revenues of the Crown. It was Gloucester's disaffection and his eventual armed withdrawal to the Marches that would lead to the outbreak of war and to the road to Evesham – and Simon's defeat and death.

The Walk

Distance: 9 miles (14.5 km)

Start at the remains of Lewes Castle (Pathfinder 1289 414101) (Point A) which stand back from the High Street. Begun by William de Warenne soon after the Conquest, the stonework of the keep dates from about 1080. The

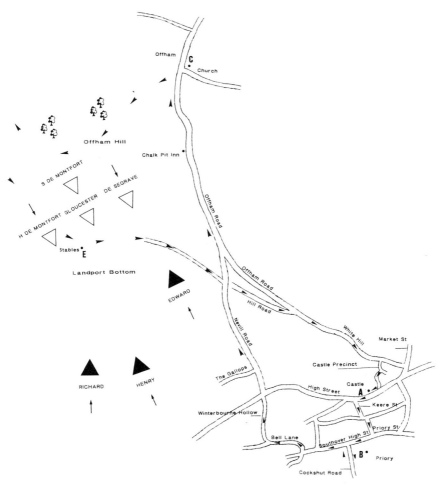

The Battle of Lewes, 1264

walls were 7 ft thick and 19 ft high from the courtyard to the wall walk. Not until the thirteenth century were the projecting towers (of which two remain) added. By ascending the southernmost of these, one can enjoy panoramic views of the surrounding countryside, particularly northward to Offham Hill. Doubtless those Royalists left behind on guard duty watched anxiously as the battle unfolded before them. Were they resentful at being denied their share of glory, or relieved at having avoided the horror of a medieval battlefield?

From the castle, turn right into High Street and then left at the town's oldest thoroughfare, Keere Street, to descend into Priory Street. Turn right into Southover High Street and left into Cockshut Lane. On the left-hand side, just beyond the small railway arch, is the entrance to the remains of the Cluniac Priory of St Pancras (Pathfinder 1308 417096) (Point B) where Henry lodged before the battle. Founded by de Warenne, it became one of the most celebrated Cluniac priories in Europe. It was destroyed at the Dissolution in 1538, a sacrilege compounded over three hundred years later by vandalism attendant upon the construction of the Lewes to Brighton railway line.

Return to Southover High Street and turn to the left. At the end, turn to the right up Bell Lane and continue bearing right up into Winterbourne Hollow, uphill along a narrow footpath raised up from the tree-lined road below. At the crossroads, continue up Nevill Road. Henry would have occupied centre position on the land occupied today by HM Prison, Lewes, ahead, with his brother, Richard, to the left and Prince Edward to the right. Early in the nineteenth century, burial pits were unearthed in the region of the gaol which would suggest that much heavy fighting occurred in this area. Continue walking up Nevill Road and out of Lewes into Offham Road (the A275) which has a footpath on the right-hand side. This is a walk of seemingly endless panoramic views, more of which crowd in on the right as gaps appear in the trees. To the left are old chalk pits, the site of more graves, and snugly tucked away among them is the aptly named Chalk Pit Inn where refreshment may be taken.

Continue to Offham, a hamlet with a church, St Peter's (unfortunately kept locked) and very little else. A clearly marked public footpath (Pathfinder 1288 400121) (Point C) branches off to the left. Follow the right-hand fork leading up to Offham Hill. There has been some debate as to the point at which Simon's rebel army broke away from the road. By leaving the road slightly to the north of Offham, a more gradual ascent to the high ground occupied by Offham Hill could have been achieved. Certainly, the climb via the chalky track is a very precipitous one for the lightly clad rambler and would have been all the more so for a heavily armed medieval knight.

Bearing right, follow the well marked path towards Mount Harry. A compass is sometimes useful on a walk such as this one when landmarks are in short supply. However, electricity pylons often constitute welcome points of reference – as they do here. The path leading up to Mount Harry strikes off to the north east, hugging the woods on the right. Much of the land is given over to sheep which are penned in by modern metal fencing. Gone, alas, are the days when one could wander carelessly over these hills and one now meets with the occasional notice reminding one that inviting short cuts are not public rights of way. As soon as one passes beneath the electricity pylons, the path broadens out and, yet again, a breathtaking vista opens out to the north.

Just before the ascent to 'Blackcap' Hill – crowned with a knot of firs commemorating the coronation of Queen Elizabeth II – one arrives at a junction (Point D). Turn sharp left here (Pathfinder 1288 377113) to embark on a gradual descent of the southern slopes of Mount Harry, perhaps named after Henry III. Walk down through the gate (where one learns that the path to Blackcap is cared for by the National Trust) and towards the racehorse stables – the site of the grandstand of the long-vanished Lewes racecourse, which marks Henry de Montfort's position (Pathfinder 1288 393111) (Point E). Bear left, skirting the stables, continuing along the track which becomes a byway. A little further on, at the fork, bear to the right. The rebel centre, under the Earl of Gloucester, would have occupied the high ground to the left. (It is worth noting that today, although for much of the walk one is only a short distance from Lewes, the town, obscured by high ground, cannot be seen.)

The byway develops into a single-track road. Off to the right is Landport Bottom, the site of the decisive infantry clash and of 'King Harry's Mill', where Richard sought refuge. Ignoring the newly established public footpath across Landport Bottom, continue to follow the road, which runs across the line of Prince Edward's advance on de Segrave's rebel Londoners. It was a brave – some would say foolhardy – action to embark on an uphill charge against an enemy occupying such a strong position. Experienced and well disciplined infantry would have punished such rashness.

Emerging into Nevill Road, cross over into Hill Road, which joins Offham Road, following it down into White Hill. A right turn into Castle Precinct takes one back to the starting point – Lewes Castle – and perhaps further refreshment at one of the town's excellent inns.

Further Explorations

The strategic importance of the surrounding area was recognized as early as the Iron Age, as the hill-fort of Mount Caburn (Landranger 198 4408) suggests. Excavations imply that at least seventy households were accommodated within the 3 acre site but it is certain that the ¼ mile long ramparts would also have afforded protection to the inhabitants of nearby villages in time of need.

Evidence of much earlier settlement may be seen a little to the north of Mount Caburn at Cliffe Hill (Landranger 198 4310), the site of a Neolithic burial mound. Remains of a supposedly even earlier Sussex resident were identified by a Lewes solicitor and amateur archaeologist, Charles Dawson, in 1911, with the discovery at Piltdown (Landranger 198 4422) near Fletching, of the infamous Piltdown Man. The find consisted of a human cranium and an ape-like jawbone which, when fitted together, constituted what Dawson claimed to be the 'Missing Link'. Although many experts doubted its authenticity from the outset, it was not until 1953 that scientific tests established beyond doubt that the supposedly ancient remains had been faked. Thus, Arthur Mee, in the first (1938) edition of his Sussex volume in the 'King's England' series, could still wax lyrical about '. . . our true ancestor . . . the oldest known inhabitant of these islands'.

To the south east of Lewes is Glynde (Landranger 198 4509) and Glynde Place, an Elizabethan mansion and home of Colonel Herbert Morley, MP for Lewes and zealous Parliamentarian during the Civil War. During the power-struggle within the army following the death of Cromwell, Morley gained momentary fame as the man who challenged the ambitious Major-General John Lambert as he marched on Westminster. Armed with a pistol, Morley blocked Lambert's path, threatening to shoot him if he took another step. Lambert retreated and, in so doing, may as well have carried on to the Tower where he was destined to begin a sentence of life imprisonment. Morley refused to sit in judgement on Charles I and therefore saved his own life, surviving to settle down to a life of peace on his estate. His remains lie close by, in St Mary's Church. On the whole, although it had its share of Royalist families ruined by heavy fines, Sussex suffered less during the Civil War than many other counties.

To the south of Glynde is Firle Place (Landranger 198 4707), with a priest's hole accessed by a window seat in the long gallery, and Firle Beacon (Landranger 198 4805), the highest point in the locality, overlooking the South Downs Way, a long-distance footpath running a distance of 106 miles between Winchester and Eastbourne.

It is worth continuing down to the coast to Seaford, where it is possible to visit a Martello tower (Landranger 198 4898), one of seventy-four such forts built – at great expense – along the south and south-east coasts during the Napoleonic wars. This strategy is said to have evolved from the problems experienced by the British in capturing Corsica, where they met with stiff resistance directed from a tower situated on Cape Mortella. The circular towers, constructed of masonry, are about 45 ft in diameter and are capped with a gun platform. Damp and dingy, they must have represented an unpopular assignment for the small garrisons allocated to them.

Further Information

Lewes does not cater for tourist traffic. A complicated one-way system, not unlike the Monaco Grand Prix circuit – and treated as such by local motorists – can hold the unwary visitor in its ugly grasp for the better part of half an hour, and car parking facilities are confined to limited waiting periods on scraps of waste land. One of the main benefits of a circular walk is that it can be joined anywhere along the way and in this case it may be preferable for motorists to take as a starting point one of several lay-bys on the A275 Offham road.

Rail travellers are well served, with trains from London (Victoria) (telephone 0171 928 5100) and also the south-coast service between Worthing and Hastings (telephone 0171 928 5100). There is no National Express coach service. The dedicated county public transport enquiry line is 01273 474747.

Ordnance Survey maps for the area are Landranger 198 and Pathfinders 1288, 1289 and 1308. Both 1289 and 1288 are essential for the walk, but a good local street map compensates more than adequately for the lack of 1308.

It is usual to purchase tickets for entry to Lewes Castle at the museum – which has nothing of specific interest for the student of the battle – opposite the entrance. (In season, parties of poorly supervised schoolchildren abound, and before purchasing one's ticket, it is as well to ensure that the castle has not fallen into their possession.) Lewes does have a Tourist Information Office, situated in the High Street (telephone 01273 483448), which should be contacted for information about up-to-date admission charges and so on.

The standard texts all include chapters on the Battle of Lewes. Particularly helpful are Seymour's *Battles in Britain 1066–1547*, which contains a useful aerial photograph of the battlefield, and Burne's *More Battlefields of England* – a splendidly irascible assessment.

5
THE BATTLE OF BARNET
14 April 1471

Introduction

The Battle of Barnet has occasionally been described as having taken place towards the end of the Wars of the Roses. However, some of the bloodiest battles – Tewkesbury (4 May 1471), Bosworth Field (22 August 1485) and Stoke Field (16 June 1487) – were yet to come, the civil wars being brought to a close only with Perkin Warbeck's abortive Yorkist-backed rising of 1497. And even then the systematic slaughter of everyone with the merest hint of Yorkist blood coursing through their veins was to continue well into the sixteenth century.

It is also a matter of some surprise that so few battles of importance occurred in the south of England during the Wars of the Roses. In addition to Barnet, there were only two others – the First Battle of St Albans, the opening encounter in the monumental struggle between the Houses of York and Lancaster which took place on 22 May 1455, and the Second Battle of St Albans, fought on 17 February 1461, which resulted in a shattering Yorkist defeat. Both St Albans' battlefields have been lost in a welter of urban development, but sufficient survives of Barnet battlefield to provide the explorer with a pleasant and instructive walk.

The Battle of Barnet was a battle of three kings and a kingmaker. The king whose claim to the throne of England many considered to be the strongest was Henry VI, who had ruled for the House of Lancaster from 1422 to 1461. In fact Henry's capacity to rule had been seriously compromised since 1453, when he suffered the first of his mental breakdowns which left him in a virtually catatonic state. His recovery late in the following year was only partial and he remained an essentially passive figure, finding comfort in a preoccupation with religion. Although present at various battles, he took no part in any of them and was shuttled back and forth between captors and allies without having the least understanding of what was happening to him. As for Henry's queen, the power-seeking Margaret of Anjou, whom he had married in 1445, the king's illness provided her with an opportunity to display a remarkable determination and ruthlessness in attempts to establish her own personal rule.

The second king present at Barnet was Edward IV, who had assumed the crown in 1461 on behalf of the House of York; this meant that for several years England had two kings, each of whom was in a position to command the allegiance of his subjects. Although only twenty years of age when he was hailed as the rival monarch, Edward profited from the support and friendship of 'the kingmaker' Richard Neville, Earl of Warwick, the wealthiest, most powerful baron in the country. At thirty-three Warwick was only thirteen years Edward's senior, but their relationship was almost as father to son.

However, there came a time when Edward wished to break loose from his mentor's influence and, had Warwick accepted this natural development and retreated gracefully into the background, it is likely that he would have retained a degree of influence, and that his family would have continued to occupy a position of prominence in the affairs of the nation for many years to come. Sadly, in his resentment of the king's desire for independence, he transferred his allegiance to the House of Lancaster and, in so doing, lost his life and destroyed a dynasty at a single stroke.

The Battle of Barnet's third monarch would have to wait another twelve years before occupying the throne – Edward's youngest brother, Richard, just eighteen years of age, was content at this time to fight by the king's side, in what was his first major engagement. And, as will be seen, this slightly built youth, who had shown but little interest in jousting and other manly pursuits, was to acquit himself well in the captain's role now entrusted to him.

The Road to Barnet

The road to Barnet was a long and slippery one. Steadily deteriorating relations between Edward IV and the Earl of Warwick reached the point of no return with Edward's choice of wife. Elizabeth Woodville, the widow of a Lancastrian knight, Sir John Grey, who had been killed fighting for the House of Lancaster at the Second Battle of St Albans, was five years Edward's senior. In some respects, she constituted a steadying influence in terms of moderating the excesses of the pleasure-loving king, but Warwick interpreted the act as a personal insult. For some time, he had been trying to match Edward with a suitable French bride and, by so doing, to isolate

Margaret of Anjou, who hoped to secure an ally in Louis XI. Not only had all his work been in vain, but the Nevilles, who had hitherto enjoyed an unchallenged monopoly of the cream of grace and favour appointments, now faced formidable competition from an ambitious rival family. When Edward's sister married Charles the Bold of Burgundy in 1468, thus further alienating France, relations between king and kingmaker deteriorated to a level which led to the outbreak of hostilities.

The period 1469–71 was a time of great instability with both parties alternately gaining the upper hand. At length, Warwick fled to France, where Queen Margaret, keen to turn the situation to her advantage, forged an alliance with her old enemy. On 13 September 1470 Warwick landed at Dartmouth at the head of an invasion force which included his brother, Clarence, the Earl of Pembroke (Jasper Tudor) and the Earl of Oxford. Caught unawares and lacking the depth of support needed to organize a challenge, Edward fled to Burgundy, where he was supplied with 2,000 men, a force which included a number of German soldiers armed with hand-guns – by no means innovative weapons, having been employed at the Second Battle of St Albans ten years earlier.

Edward returned to England on 14 March 1471, landing at Ravenspur, near Hull, to find Warwick and his own brother, Clarence, ensconced as joint protectors of the realm, for although Henry had been restored to the throne, it was argued that he was incapable of taking an active role in government. On landing, Edward hurried to York where, much to his relief, he was admitted by the citizens. As far as his immediate prospects were concerned, the significance of his acceptance by the second most important city in the kingdom cannot be over-emphasized. On Tuesday 19 March his army, somewhat refreshed and growing in confidence, commenced its march southward, adding to its numbers along the way. John Neville, Lord Montague, Warwick's brother and the victor of the Battle of Hexham (1464), could have challenged its progress at Pontefract, and may have done so but for his unease at the degree of support Edward appeared to be commanding.

Warwick also was far from confident of his own strength. At the end of March 1471, he was recruiting in Warwickshire when he learned that Edward was advancing towards him from Nottingham. Warwick retreated, along with some 6,000 followers, inside the city walls of Coventry. Arriving on the scene, Edward offered battle but Warwick refused, preferring to wait for Clarence whose army was approaching from the West Country. While making it plain that he was prepared to fight if necessary, Edward let it be known that his preferred option was to welcome back 'false, fleeting, perjur'd Clarence' to the fold. In response, when the brothers met, Clarence threw himself on Edward's mercy, and the two armies were amalgamated.

Although he had been offered his life, Warwick stubbornly refused to submit. Instead of assaulting the city, Edward decided that it would be wiser to continue on his southward march to London, gambling on winning the citizens' support. In fact, the citizens were in a difficult position, for they had received two sets of instructions: one set from Edward, ordering them to prepare for his arrival, and a second from Warwick, instructing them to hold the city on his behalf for two or three days. Edward guessed that their support would go to whoever arrived first, and he intended to win the race. In a misguided attempt to win support for Warwick, his other brother, George Neville, Archbishop of York, paraded the feeble Henry VI, dressed in a shabby blue gown, through the streets – a sight which would have done little for the Lancastrian cause.

On 11 April Edward reached the city walls and, as expected, was welcomed by the Londoners who, instead of offering opposition, were content to admit him via Bishopsgate. Almost immediately, Henry VI and George Neville were confined to the Tower, and when word spread that Edward had reasserted his authority, more troops flocked to his banner.

Meanwhile, Warwick's own march to London had been hampered by a rearguard action which succeeded in keeping him about 20 miles behind Edward's army. When he learned that Edward had entered London unopposed, he decided to stake everything on one decisive battle. When he halted at St Albans, it seemed that the town would host its third battle but, in the event, he removed his army a distance of 10 miles, to what was described as a 'faire plaine' outside Barnet, known today as Hadley Green.

The Battle of Barnet

Warwick deployed his men in three divisions. Montague, who had decided to throw in his lot with his brother, commanded the centre, with Henry Holland, Duke of Exeter, on the left and John de Vere, Earl of Oxford, on the right. Warwick himself was in the rear, in command of the reserve.

Edward, too, was anxious to bring matters to a speedy conclusion, and on 13 April 1471, Easter Saturday, with Henry VI in tow, he marched out to meet the 'rebel' Lancastrian army, even though, in essence, the issue was one of Yorkist against Yorkist. He reached Barnet towards nightfall and, determined to fight on the following day, advanced beyond the settlement to take up battle positions, a task rendered difficult by thick fog. As far as he was able, and under fire from Warwick's artillery, he matched his own three divisions with those of the rebels. William, Lord Hastings, commanded the left, Edward led the centre and Richard, Duke of Gloucester, took command of the right. Nowhere is it stated that a reserve existed, although the existence of one cannot be ruled out.

The Battle of Barnet, from a
contemporary manuscript.
(Bridgeman Art Library)

In terms of comparative strength of arms, estimates vary, contemporary chroniclers setting rebel numbers as high as 30,000. It is generally accepted that the balance was in Warwick's favour – perhaps 15,000 rebels to Edward's 12,000. However, this reckoning may take insufficient account of the numbers flocking to Edward's banner, following his acceptance at York and London. It is also possible that a number of rebels slipped away during the night under cover of the fog. In reality, therefore, the protagonists may have been quite evenly matched.

It is said that the armies were so close that the sound of men's voices was carried on the mist-laden air from one camp to the other, and neither side can have benefited from much sleep. Certainly, at 5.00 a.m. on Easter Sunday, Edward was ready to fight and commenced hostilities proper with a barrage of arrows. Shooting into the slowly clearing mist as they were, it is doubtful whether the archers succeeded in inflicting much more damage than the artillery which was also brought into play, and it was necessary at a comparatively early stage for men to come to grips in hand-to-hand combat.

As both sides advanced, it became apparent that the fog had caused Edward to miscalculate. His line overlapped Warwick's and Gloucester found himself advancing on a non-existent position. Similarly, Hastings was out of alignment with Oxford's division and the latter's advance over reasonably level ground developed naturally into an outflanking manoeuvre which put the Yorkist left wing to flight. Oxford experienced some difficulty in controlling the pursuit, and the cut-throat element embarked on a rampage which saw the Yorkists chased half-way to London. Survivors who reached the city brought stories of a wholesale Yorkist collapse, which threw the citizens into a panic. Had they, after all, backed the wrong side? Meanwhile, on the Yorkist right wing, Gloucester also found himself advancing upon vacant land, and so he turned to outflank Exeter's division – a movement lacking the punch of Oxford's because he was marching uphill, and Exeter was better able to hold his ground.

In the centre, Edward was forced to give ground. The overall effect, with Oxford and Hastings absent from the field and with Gloucester pressing in on the rebel left, was to shift the axis of the fight from north–south to east–west. At this stage Warwick must have felt that victory was within his grasp but, if so, then his hopes were to be dashed by the return of Oxford and his partly regrouped command. In the mist, Oxford, unaware of the new battle lines, approached what he thought was the Yorkist rear, but which was, in fact, Montague's right flank. Montague's men, similarly confused, bombarded Oxford's contingent with a hail of arrows. Raising cries of treason, and convinced that Montague had turned traitor, Oxford, followed by Somerset, abandoned the field for the second and last time.

Hard upon the heels of this disaster there occurred the death of Montague himself, who may have been cut down in the confusion by one of Warwick's men. With Exeter seriously wounded, Warwick was left in sole command of a rapidly disintegrating army. According to some reports, he sold his life dearly by rushing into the thickest of the fray. Others contend that he tried to flee but became entangled in a copse, where he was surrounded and killed. Yet another story describes his capture and Edward's unsuccessful attempt to save him before he was murdered by the Yorkist rank and file.

The battle had lasted about six hours. Certainly, it was over by noon and the outcome may have been decided as much as two hours earlier. Edward had won a great victory, but the real test of his ability as a leader was yet to come in his handling of people and events in the aftermath.

The Aftermath

The total number of dead may have been as many as 3,000 or as few as 1,500. Edward instructed his men to give no quarter to the enemy, and large numbers of rebel wounded must have been dispatched. The Earl of Exeter may have been wounded as early as 7.00 a.m. Left for dead, he was discovered by a retainer and provided with rudimentary medical care which fitted him for four years' imprisonment in the Tower. Oxford made good his escape, surviving to fight alongside Henry Tudor at Bosworth (1485). Somerset took the field again at Tewkesbury (1471) and was beheaded immediately afterwards. On the Yorkist side, Richard of Gloucester had been slightly wounded, while lords Cromwell and Saye and Sir Humphrey Bouchier were all killed. Some of the nobles, as well as the common soldiers, were buried locally in mass graves.

According to Gerhard von Wesel, a Hanseatic merchant then residing in England, many of the survivors were in a pitiable condition. Although body armour was effective in protecting the torso, combatants often sustained disfiguring facial wounds, and von Wesel was able to report that those who had set out sound in body returned home with mutilated faces – some without noses – as a result of which they afterwards stayed indoors.

After taking refreshment in Barnet, Edward returned to London, taking with him Henry VI, the latter clad in the same blue gown he had worn when led through the streets by George Neville. At first, with the arrival of fugitives from the beaten Yorkist right wing, it was believed in London that Warwick must be the victor, which gave rise to some rioting. The messenger whom Edward sent with news of the Yorkist success was not believed, and it was only the appearance of Edward himself that set the citizens' minds at rest. The king first went to St Paul's Cathedral, to be received by the Archbishop of Canterbury and several senior clergy, including the bishops of Bath, Lincoln and Durham. The remains of Warwick and Montague were brought to the capital and put on show in two simple wooden coffins in St Paul's so that their demise could not be doubted. Afterwards, the bodies were sent to Bisham Abbey in Berkshire, where they were interred in the family tomb. Despite the public display and subsequent burial, it was later claimed that the kingmaker was still alive, a rumour promulgated by the late earl's nephew, Thomas Neville, the 'Bastard of Fauconberg'.

Edward was keen to have it known that he regretted Warwick's death, even though the latter's survival would have constituted an embarrassment. At best, Warwick would have been consigned to the Tower, perhaps to meet the same end as Henry who was put to death there the following month. In the person of the earl, the Neville family, a force to be reckoned with, had reached the pinnacle of power. Although the Neville star would rise again, briefly, with the marriage between Warwick's daughter, Anne Neville, and Richard, Duke of Gloucester, the death of the man who has been called 'the last of the Barons', brought to an end the heady years of his family's power and influence.

In the short term, more pressing matters were engaging Edward's attention: on the day of his victory at Barnet, Queen Margaret landed at Weymouth and the Countess of Warwick at Portsmouth. On receiving news of her husband's fate, the countess fled to Beaulieu Abbey and Margaret to Cerne Abbey, where she was persuaded by the Duke of Somerset that all was not lost. Had Warwick waited for Margaret's arrival, it is probable that an army large enough to overwhelm Edward's force would have been raised, but Somerset managed to convince her that a victory in the field was yet possible, and so she embarked on the road that would take her to Tewkesbury – and final defeat.

The Walk

Distance: 5 miles (8.05 km)

Begin at the southern tip of Hadley Green (Pathfinder 1140 246970) (Point A). Walk into Hadley Green and take the footpath off to the right, a little way beyond East View. This path soon broadens out into a wide, grass track. Here, Edward IV's men were ranged out facing north. Immediately

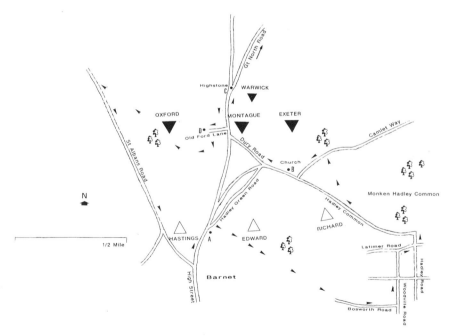

The Battle of Barnet, 1471

one becomes aware of the uneven nature of the ground, sloping away towards the trees. Follow the well worn path down. (On a clear day, the Post Office Tower is visible on the skyline to the south.) After a straight run, the path twists to the left and crosses a stream. Traverse the final field to emerge on Bosworth Road. As one makes one's way up to Monken Hadley Common, one should note the Ricardian connotations – the block of flats thoughtfully named 'Sandford' for instance, after the field at Bosworth in which Richard III met his death.

At the end of Bosworth Road, turn left into Woodville Road. Subsequent right and left turns into Latimer Road and Hadley Road respectively will bring one out on to Hadley Common. Turn left and cross over the road so as to walk along the common's perimeter. Prohibitions on public activities (including kite-flying) seem hardly necessary as much of the common today comprises impenetrable shrubbery. However, it does open out towards the end. Just before it does so, Gloucester's contingent would have been drawn up, straddling the road, his right wing somewhat hampered by the ground which falls away quite sharply. At the time of the battle, far more of the present-day common would have constituted open land, but it is over today's relatively limited open portion that Gloucester would most probably have passed.

Therefore, following in Gloucester's footsteps, walk across the common to Camlet Way. Warwick's position lay beyond the war memorial tucked away in the trees. Turn left into Camlet Way and bear right to arrive at the church of St Mary the Virgin (Pathfinder 1140 250975) (Point B). Built in 1494 (the date is given in 'half-eights' above the west door) possibly on the site of a Norman hermitage, St Mary's has many features of interest. One particularly intriguing aspect is the beacon on top of the tower which may well have been lit to warn of the approach of the Spanish Armada. It is said that the beacon was also lit by Warwick on the night before the Battle of Barnet to guide his supporters to his camp. If so, then there must have been a beacon in place twenty-three years before rebuilding was undertaken. According to another unsubstantiated story, Edward IV (who died in 1483) was responsible for the establishment of the new church in commemoration for those who fell in the battle. St Mary's is also particularly rich in brasses, although one's favourites may well be the modest effigies of William Tornor (who died in 1500) and his wife, Joan, affixed to the south wall. Fortunate are those visitors with the foresight to have packed their brass-rubbing materials – and, of course, to have obtained the permission of the rector to enable them to indulge their interest.

Leaving the church, turn right and then right again into Dury Road. At the top, another right turn leads into Hadley High Stone and, a little way along, to either the Old Windmill Inn or the King William IV Inn for refreshment. Both public houses may well occupy an area which constituted

The battlefield monument (which doubles as a milestone) known as Hadley High Stone, stands to the north of the Lancastrian position. It is one of several locations in the area where it is alleged that the Earl of Warwick met his death.

the centre of Somerset's battle. A little way further along the road is the High Stone (Pathfinder 1140 246979) (Point C), serving both as a milestone and as a monument to the Battle of Barnet. This is one of a number of sites where it has been suggested Warwick was killed. After examining the High Stone, cross to the other side of the road and walk south towards Barnet. Turn into Old Fold Lane and walk down to the clubhouse of the Old Ford Manor golf course (Pathfinder 1140 244976) (Point D). The present-day house was built in the mid-eighteenth century and stands on the site of a thirteenth-century predecessor. The Frowyke family lived there at the time of the battle and one wonders how the family reacted as the house was engulfed by Oxford's men. Were they at home? Was the manor requisitioned? Did the wounded seek shelter there?

Follow the path to the left of the clubhouse. At the point where it forks into three, choose the right-hand prong to walk through the trees and on to the golf course. As the vista opens out, one can discern the line of the old manor house moat to the rear of the clubhouse. Strike out for the clump of trees to the north west (at '2 o'clock', for those not in possession of a compass), from where the footpath running across the golf course is quite well indicated by modern signs and old black and white marker posts. From the vantage point of the golf course, one can begin to appreciate the strength of Warwick's position, his troops stretching along the ridge, looking down towards Barnet and Edward's army.

Continue to follow the path towards the A1081 which can be glimpsed at the western perimeter of the golf course. Some care is needed in negotiating the stile as there is precious little grass verge bordering the road. Again with care, cross over to the footpath on the opposite side and walk down towards Barnet. As one enters Barnet, the church on the left-hand side of the road may mark the position of Hastings' left wing. At the junction, turn sharp left into the High Street and, ultimately, the Great North Road to return to Hadley Green and the starting point. While doing so, one might reflect on the number of important battles fought along the line of the Great North Road throughout the centuries: Boroughbridge (1322), Empingham (1470), Barnet (1471), Pinkie (1547), Dunbar (1650) and Prestonpans (1745), to name but a few.

Further Explorations

Considering the importance of London for almost two thousand years, it is remarkable that so few battles have been fought in its proximity. In AD 60 Boadicea destroyed the sizeable town established by the Romans and in 886, according to the *Anglo-Saxon Chronicle*, Alfred drove out the Danes. As a general rule, however, despite bouts of civil unrest, the capital's experience of warfare has been limited – until the Blitz of 1940. But as far as Hertfordshire is concerned, there are relevant sites of interest within reasonable travelling distance of Barnet. Berkhamsted Castle (Landranger 165 9908), built in the eleventh century by Robert de Mortain, half-brother to William the Conqueror, was already in ruins by 1647 when Cromwell's troops were quartered on the site. In earlier centuries, the castle had been a favourite residence of Royalty and nobility. King John of France was imprisoned here after his capture at Poitiers in 1356.

Hertford itself had first been fortified by the Saxons, on a site by the River Lea which was later developed into a Norman castle (Landranger 166 3221), only a small portion of which has survived modernization in subsequent centuries. The year 1647 was a difficult one for Oliver Cromwell, facing widespread discontent from within the ranks of the New Model Army. Cromwell and Fairfax may have lodged at the castle in November 1647 when quelling mutiny among troops in the town. The ringleaders of the mutiny, sentenced to death by court martial, were forced to cast lots to decide who would die, not an uncommon procedure in such cases, and tantamount to be tried twice.

If further explorations are to be made in the county, then St Albans must be given some priority. The Roman town of Verulamium, sacked by Boadicea after London, is to the west of the city centre (Landranger 166 1307). As citizens of a *municipium*, residents had the same rights as citizens of Rome. A visit should be made to the Verulamium Museum and amphitheatre.

Unusually, St Albans hosted two battles during the Wars of the Roses. The First Battle of St Albans took place on 22 May 1455 and a plaque at the corner of St Peter's Street and Victoria Street commemorates the death in battle of the Duke of Somerset. Henry VI planted the Lancastrian standard to the north of the market place, in St Peter's Street. Richard, Duke of York, demanded the delivery into Yorkist hands of the Duke of Somerset, whom he blamed for the nation's ills. When Henry refused, Richard attacked, overwhelming the Lancastrians by sheer weight of numbers. The course of the Second Battle of St Albans of 17 February 1461 is more difficult to follow, with much of the fighting taking place outside the medieval town on open land, long since urbanized. On this occasion, the Yorkists under the Earl of Warwick were routed, many of the dead being interred in a mass grave in St Peter's churchyard.

During the Civil War, Roundhead troops were frequently stationed in the town. On 14 January 1643 Cromwell broke up a Royalist meeting in the market-place and arrested Sir Thomas Coningsby, the High Sheriff of Hertfordshire, who was in the process of reading a Royal proclamation. The quartering of troops in the town gave rise to complaints from the inhabitants to the effect that the hospitality they were compelled to offer went unrecompensed. St Albans Abbey was also requisitioned for use as a conference hall and court. Here, Nathaniel Fiennes, Parliamentarian Governor of Bristol, was tried and sentenced to death for surrendering the seaport to Prince Rupert in July 1943 (see p. 117). In November 1648 a Council of Officers meeting in the abbey approved Ireton's 'Remonstrance of the Army' which called for the king to be brought to justice and for the abolition of the monarchy.

Further Information

Barnet is within easy reach of the centre of London, so there is no reason why Londoners should not enjoy a battlefield walk. If travelling within London, then one can easily reach the site via High Barnet station on London Underground's Northern Line. For details of both underground and London bus services, telephone 0171 222 1234. If travelling into

London by rail, it is as well to continue to the main line terminus and travel out to Barnet by bus or underground. There is no National Express coach service to Barnet.

Motorists travelling via the M25 should take exit 23 for the A1081 St Albans Road into Barnet. Filter in to the first left turn, Dancer's Hill Road, and follow it down to the end. Turn right into the A1000 Great North Road. 'Deadman's Bottom' is situated on the left shortly after the turn. The 'Highstone' monument is further down on the right. Parking is available on the roadside by Monken Hadley Green.

A detailed account of the battle and of events leading up to it may be found in P.W. Hammond's *Battlefields of Barnet and Tewkesbury*. Useful chapters may also be found in Burne's *Battlefields of England* and Seymour's *Battles in Britain 1066–1547*.

It will be noted that much of the recommended reading throughout this book constitutes secondary source material. This is because the matter of accessibility has been taken into account. Even some of the most interesting secondary sources may be difficult to acquire. For example, a splendid account of the Battle of Barnet was produced by Frederick Charles Cass, Rector of Monken Hadley from 1860 to 1890, in the January 1882 issue of the *Transactions of the London and Middlesex Archaeological Society*. A copy is available via the Barton Library for perusal by members of the Richard III Society, but non-members of the society will find its acquisition a little more difficult. However, some readily available primary source material may be introduced in the shape of the Paston Letters – the largest surviving collection of fifteenth-century letters in England – concerning correspondence between members of the Paston family of Norfolk, one of whom was wounded fighting for Warwick at Barnet. For a very readable commentary, see *The Pastons: a family in the Wars of the Roses*, ed. Richard Barber.

Ordnance Survey maps covering the area are Landranger 176 and Pathfinder 1140, although a London A–Z Street Atlas is an invaluable asset. A locally available publication, *Monken Hadley Church and Village* by W.H. Gelder, will also prove a useful companion.

6
THE BATTLE OF LANSDOWN
5 July 1643

Introduction

In the opening campaign of the English Civil War, King Charles appointed William Seymour, the Marquess of Hertford, as his Lieutenant-General in the West. Hertford was accompanied by Sir Ralph Hopton. A one-time reformer who, as MP for Wells and Somerset, had supported Parliament's efforts to limit the king's power, Hopton had stopped short of rebellion and thrown in his lot with the Royalists. Necessarily, Hertford's initial concern lay with recruitment, and in this he was up against it with Somerset's perennially depressed clothing industry and rampant non-conformity ensuring that the Parliamentary cause received strong support. At the end of the day, retaining only a few hundred recruits, Hertford crossed the Bristol Channel into Glamorganshire, where he met with more success, later moving on into the West Midlands. Hopton, who seems to have fallen out with Hertford at an early stage, pushed on into Devon and Cornwall where, with the aid of Sir Bevil Grenville, he too was more successful. Like Hopton, Grenville had started out as a reformist but had changed sides to lead the Cornish infantry – whose mettle would not be found wanting in the fighting to come.

Prominent among the Roundhead commanders in the west during the early stages of the Civil War were the Earl of Stamford and Sir Arthur Hesilrige. Stamford's career was destined to be short-lived: while stalking Hopton in Cornwall on 19 January 1643, he was drawn into a trap at Braddock Down and put to flight. Although he redeemed himself somewhat at Sir James Chudleigh's victory over the Royalists at Sourton Down on 25 April 1643, he himself was again defeated – largely owing to the bravery of Grenville's pike-men – the following month at Stratton.

Sir Arthur Hesilrige became famous for raising his own regiment of cuirassiers, nicknamed 'Lobsters' because of the full body armour which they wore, and which rendered them virtually impervious to injury in the normal course of combat. Eccentric, yet bold in battle, Hesilrige became a fixture in William Waller's army when Waller was appointed Major-General in the West. In the great tradition of British generals, Waller himself was a sound tactician, though perhaps lacking the killer-instinct which transforms competence into genius. Before the war, Waller and Hopton had been close friends, having served together as gentlemen volunteers in the Palatinate in the 1620s. Throughout the war, despite confrontations between their respective armies, they kept up an amicable correspondence.

While there is no indication that Waller and Hesilrige were friendly, at least they were able to work together. As far as Hertford and Hopton were concerned, however, as already suggested, there had been mutual ill-feeling from the outset, and they would never learn to cooperate. A further potential complication to the line of command in the campaign leading up to the battles of Lansdown and Roundway Down was the presence of Prince Maurice, nominally Hertford's Lieutenant-General of Horse but accustomed to acting very much as he pleased. Thus, while it is easy to criticize Hertford for his failings, one should not underestimate the difficulties he faced in managing his senior personnel.

At this stage in the proceedings, all the significant action seemed to be taking place away from the west, in the struggle for the North Sea ports and

The contribution of Prince Maurice, the younger brother of Prince Rupert, to the Royalist war effort is often underrated. The many significant engagements in which he participated include the first battle of the Civil War, at Powick Bridge (1642), Lansdown and Roundway Down (1643), the Second Battle of Newbury (1643), Lostwithiel (1644) and Naseby (1645). (Ashmolean Museum)

the industrial base of the West Midlands. The coming campaign, particularly as far as the Royalist High Command was concerned, would change all this, with the transformation of the West Country from side-show to main attraction.

The Road to Lansdown

Hopton's victory at Stratton on 16 May 1643 led to Parliamentarian fears of a Royalist advance out of the extreme south west into Dorset and beyond. Reaching a similar conclusion, King Charles decided to strengthen Hopton's infantry with a body of horse and to this end sent the Marquess of Hertford and Prince Maurice to join him. Although advised to nip this stratagem in the bud by barring Hertford's progress at Salisbury, Waller instead marched to Royalist-held Worcester which he besieged on 29 May. His reasons for taking this course of action are unclear. Certainly Worcester could be seen both as the key to the River Severn and as an important gateway to the west in terms of the road network. Nevertheless, the town defences proved too strong and Waller, under strong pressure to return to the south west, withdrew his mauled army. His absence enabled Hertford to link up with Hopton at Chard in Somerset, making a total force of well in excess of 6,000 men comprising about 2,000 horse, 4,000 foot and 300 dragoons. On 8 June Waller reached Bath. On 10 June a minor cavalry engagement at Chewton Mendip, one of a number of inconclusive skirmishes, led to Prince Maurice falling into enemy hands. Fortunately, he was not recognized and the Earl of Carnarvon engineered his rescue.

Although strengthened by the arrival of Hesilrige's cuirassiers, Waller was still short of infantry, his main problem being lack of money to pay his men. Unlike Cromwell, who broke up mutinous grumbling by wading in, sword drawn, among the recalcitrants, Waller usually contented himself with formal complaints to Parliament. He managed to beg a few hundred men from the Bristol garrison, which gave him a maximum of 1,500 foot soldiers. While he was making frantic efforts to augment his force, he was still corresponding regularly with Hopton, thanks to which many prisoners were exchanged.

On 2 July the Royalists marched out from their base at Wells and occupied Bradford-upon-Avon in readiness for an assault on Bath. Thus pressed into action, Waller moved out to Claverton Down, 2 miles to the east of the old town, where he deployed his men. An advance party of horse and foot under Colonel Robert Burghill was sent out over the River Avon to harry the approaching Royalists. Burghill succeeded in ambushing the enemy force in woodland at Monkton Farleigh but as more Royalist troops came up in support, he was forced to withdraw to the river and a previously fortified crossing point near Claverton House. A Royalist cavalry charge took the crossing only to find that Burghill had rejoined Waller who was now retreating to Bath.

The Royalist command appreciated the importance of taking Lansdown Hill, but decided to delay such a move until the following morning. Although they were on the move well before dawn, they found that Waller had beaten them to it in a night-time manoeuvre which had gone undetected even by those Royalists who had pitched their tents beneath the promontory. Lieutenant-Colonel Walter Slingsby of Lord Mohun's Royalist Regiment of Foot was moved to describe Waller as a 'shifter and chooser of ground' and it was for such nocturnal activity that Waller earned the nickname 'Night Owl'. A general panic ensued, with the Royalist vanguard, including Slingsby, harassed by Waller's artillery, retreating to join the main body; this move was followed in the early afternoon by an orderly withdrawal of the entire Royalist army to Marshfield. Although Waller had inflicted no serious damage on the enemy, he had led them a merry dance and, in the process, had succeeded in raising the morale of his own outnumbered force.

The Battle of Lansdown

On the morning of 5 July 1643 Waller shifted his position from the southern to the northern end of Lansdown and began to construct breastworks as cover for his infantry. Concealed in woodland on both flanks were musketeers. Hopton, meanwhile, was assembling his army on Tog Hill, 1½ miles to the north east.

Such fighting as occurred during the better part of the day was limited to skirmishes between opposing parties of dragoons, notably in the area of Freezing Hill. By mid-afternoon the Royalist horse was very much on the defensive, having been beaten back to the foot of Tog Hill. As usual, there was a shortage of ammunition and Hopton retreated once more towards Marshfield.

At this juncture, Waller made an extraordinary decision, dispatching a force of cavalry and dragoons – in total around 800 men – to charge the retreating Royalists, a tactic which initially created confusion in the enemy ranks, the Royalist horse recoiling on their own infantry. The situation was saved for the Royalists by units of Cornish musketeers (deployed, it would appear, on the orders of Prince Maurice) who held their ground until such time as the Earl of Carnarvon's Regiment of Horse was able to mount a

Royalist counter-charge. Despite being wounded in the action, Carnarvon managed to turn the Roundheads, who started to fall back towards their main lines.

With most of the Royalist horse in retreat and his own position on Tog Hill coming under Roundhead cannon fire, Hopton decided the time was ripe for an assault on Lansdown. Horse and infantry began a steady advance on Waller's centre, while flanking parties of musketeers advanced on the woods to left and right. Sir Bevil Grenville's regiment, leading the assault, came under heavy fire, but the cover afforded by hedges and walls meant that initially their casualties were light. When they reached the brow of the hill, however, their lines were raked by case-shot and musket volleys. Several fierce cavalry charges led by Hesilrige and Waller himself resulted in Grenville's death, but failed to blunt the attack. A particularly graphic account of the action was given by Royalist Captain Richard Atkyns: '. . . the air was so darkened by the smoke of the powder, that for a quarter of an hour together (I dare say) there was no light seen, but what the fire of the volleys of shot gave; and 'twas the greatest storm that ever I saw, in which though I knew not whither to go, nor what to do.' Atkyns adds that Grenville's pike-men, though without their leader, were still playing a significant role, standing 'as upon the eaves of an house for steepness, but as unmoveable as a rock'.

Sir Bevil Grenville's monument at Lansdown, now in the care of English Heritage – and in need of some restoration.

As the battle wore on through the late afternoon and into the early evening, Hopton's numerical strength began to tell. After some heavy fighting in the woods, the Royalist musketeers broke through on both flanks and light artillery was brought up, forcing Waller to abandon the breastworks. A sheepcote surrounded by a high stone wall lay to the rear and he took cover behind this.

With the day drawing to a close – it was now after 8.00 p.m. – and both sides battle-weary, the fighting subsided into a long-range musket duel in which the Royalists, struggling to consolidate their position on the brow of the hill, were at a disadvantage. The onset of darkness saved them from severe punishment, although they were kept pinned down in the hollows where they had sought shelter throughout what remained of the evening by vigilant Roundhead musket fire.

Both sides went in fear of a night attack for, as was customary in such stand-off situations, both sides thought they had lost. At about 1.00 a.m. Prince Maurice discerned that Waller was on the move. An unexpected musket volley suggested that Waller was, indeed, about to launch an assault. After an hour, all remained quiet, and a Royalist scout reported that the Roundheads had withdrawn, leaving lit matches along the top of the stone wall and pikes standing upright, so as to give the impression that the defences were still manned. In fact Waller was already on the road to Bath, leaving the field to Hopton and enabling him, with some justification, to claim the victory.

The Aftermath

At first light the Royalists assumed control of Waller's abandoned position, recovering several hundred weapons. As might be expected, casualties, especially among the Royalists, were high. It was said that of 2,000 Royalist cavalry, less than 600 remained. However, as Captain Atkyns ruefully remarked, many Cavaliers had fled during the assault on the hill, so it can by no means be presumed that 1,400 perished.

At length Hopton retired to Tog Hill, where some enemy prisoners had been placed in an ammunition cart containing several barrels of gunpowder. As Hopton approached, one of the prisoners lit a pipe and dropped a match among the barrels. The resulting explosion, which could be heard in Bath, killed or injured many who were in proximity to the wagon, including Hopton who was left temporarily blinded and paralysed.

While Waller's men stocked up with fresh supplies, including sixty barrels of gunpowder, the Royalists made their way disconsolately to Marshfield and from there to Chippenham. Suitably provisioned and reinforced, Waller set off in pursuit, arriving within striking distance in the late afternoon of 8 July. At first it seemed as though the weary Royalists might be coaxed into a fight close to the town. Instead, the following day Hertford and Prince Maurice decided to fall back on Devizes, a costly but successful rearguard action enabling them to achieve their objective. With the Royalists penned in, Waller proceeded to install himself on Roundway Hill, 2 miles to the north of the town. In effect, Devizes was under siege.

On the evening of 10 July Hertford, Prince Maurice and Hopton decided that the latter, still seriously incapacitated, would remain in Devizes with the Royalist infantry, while Hertford and Prince Maurice made a 40 mile dash for Oxford to get reinforcements. At midnight the cavalry broke out unchallenged, Waller being preoccupied with the interception of a Royalist relief column under the command of the Earl of Crawford, sent out from Bristol. The column was routed and five precious ammunition waggons taken.

For the next three days, Waller subjected Devizes to a continuous artillery bombardment. Then, on Thursday 13 July he received reports of another relief force approaching from Marlborough. Hastily assembled by Prince Maurice, it comprised three brigades commanded by Sir John Byron, Lord Wilmot and the Earl of Crawford. Although now facing the besieger's nightmare scenario of being trapped between a relief force and the garrison he was investing, Waller, with some 2,000 horse and 2,500 infantry, enjoyed a measure of numerical superiority.

Waller deployed his men to the north of the town, between Roundway Hill and King's Play Hill, his infantry in the centre flanked by cavalry commanded by Hesilrige on the right and Waller himself on the left. It had been part of the Royalist plan for Hopton's infantry, at a prearranged gunshot signal, to attack the Roundhead rear. Fearing that Waller's withdrawal might be a ruse to draw him out, Hopton refused to move. Wilmot, leading the Royalist force, decided that the best way to proceed was to attack regardless. A 'forlorn hope', dispatched by Waller to harass the advancing Royalists, was quickly put to flight by a concentrated cavalry charge. Hesilrige, possibly on his own authority, led his cuirassiers forward to lend support to the retreating force but they were met head-on by Wilmot's more manoeuvrable cavalry, and after a sharp encounter were compelled to give ground and finally to quit the field altogether. The encounter between Waller and Sir John Byron which followed had a similar result, the furious Royalist charge forcing the Roundheads back on their own reserves. Fleeing for their lives, many of the pursued came to grief in the rapid descent of a steep, concealed escarpment.

Rallying as many of his horse as possible, Wilmot now tried to break the Roundhead infantry ranks which, under Waller's personal direction, withstood several charges. Only when Hopton's infantry appeared below them, advancing at long last from Devizes, did Waller withdraw, an initially orderly retreat disintegrating with the hurried departure of the officers and anyone who could lay his hands upon a horse's bridle. Left to fend for themselves, the Roundhead infantry were picked off by Wilmot's pursuing cavalry. Probably in excess of three hundred were killed, with several hundred more being taken prisoner.

Waller returned to Bath, having lost the battle, his army and, as far as his critics were concerned, his credibility. In a little over one week, he had transformed a threatening situation into a particularly promising one, only to have the final victory, in what should have been his finest hour, torn cruelly from his grasp. Such are the fortunes of war. On 26 July Bristol fell to the Marquess of Hertford and the West Country became a Royalist stronghold for the duration of the conflict.

The Walk

Distance: 3½ miles (5.63 km)

Begin at the Grenville Monument (Pathfinder 1167 722704) (Point A) on Lansdown Hill, near the junction of Bath Road and Freezinghill Lane. The monument itself, sited among the trees about 100 yards from the road, was erected by Grenville's grandson and is noted by Barrett in *Battles and Battlefields of England* (published in 1896) as being in a state of 'fairly good preservation'. Restoration work was carried out in 1955 but at the time of writing (1995) it would appear that further work is required.

From the monument, do not turn back to the road. Instead follow the path – the Cotswold Way – in an easterly direction on a course which takes one first downhill towards the area identified on Pathfinder 1167 as 'The Battlefields', before swinging back up, following the field pattern, to cross the eastern tip of Lansdown. The area one overlooks at this point would have been quite thickly wooded in 1643 and would have witnessed musketry duels between the defenders and Hopton's left wing flanking party. Follow the path around to the right, hugging the field perimeter. On reaching the single-track road, walk on to rejoin Bath Road. Waller's final position (the site of the stone wall to which he retreated) would have been in the immediate vicinity, marginally to the north or south. However, turn right on to Bath Road and walk back in the direction of the monument.

Immediately before the wood on the left (Beach Wood), the Cotswold Way branches off. Take this track and follow it between the trees and the

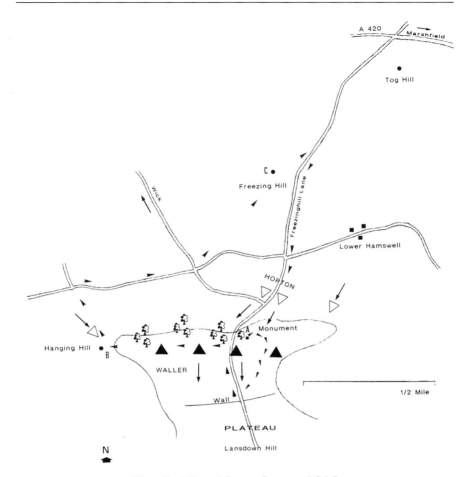

The Battle of Lansdown, 1643

field towards Hanging Hill. Walk past the wireless mast (Pathfinder 1167 717703), still following the Cotswold Way, to Hanging Hill itself, Lansdown's precipitous westernmost edge, where three paths meet (Pathfinder 1167 712702) (Point B). Turn right and descend Hanging Hill via the single-track road. Hopton's flanking musketeers approaching Waller's left wing would have endured a steep enough climb. At Hanging Hill Cottages (Pathfinder 1167 710706) turn right.

Walk to the crossroads. Cross over (again, with care) and take the footpath (Pathfinder 1167 718707) leading up to Freezing Hill. At first, the path runs almost parallel with the Lower Hamswell road, but the road falls away and the footpath continues straight ahead in a steep ascent of the hill. At the top of the hill, the path crosses an earthwork (Pathfinder 1167 722712), suggesting that the area may have witnessed the clash of primitive arms many centuries before the protagonists of the Battle of Lansdown appeared on the scene. The path strikes off diagonally over the crest of the hill (Point C) from which the Royalists launched their attack, having marched from Tog Hill, which can be seen 1 mile away to the north.

Aim for the right-hand corner of the field ahead, where the path exits on to Freezinghill Lane. Turn right to follow the course of the Royalists as they marched on under continuous fire from the heights of Lansdown. (The busy Bath Road between the junction with Freezinghill Lane (Pathfinder 1167 723705) and the monument is quite narrow, so extra care should be taken.) The lower slopes would have afforded some measure of protection but, as one follows in Captain Atkyns' footsteps, one recalls his observations concerning the dead and dying troops and the fleeing horsemen he passed as he struggled on. Gaining the plateau, one may pause for breath, unlike Grenville's infantrymen who were met immediately with concentrated artillery and musket fire. One can only marvel at the determination which won them a foothold on the plateau before forcing Waller back to the cover of the wall. To the right is the monument, which must be very near the spot where Grenville fell.

At 3½ miles the walk is short but also demanding in view of the hills which have to be negotiated. For this reason, the absence en route of a public house where one may seek refreshment is regrettable.

Further Explorations

Three miles to the north of the battlefield is Dyrham Park (Pathfinder 1167 745760) which was built for William Blathwayt, Secretary of State to William III. The mansion, its gardens and deer park, are now owned by the National Trust. Dyrham was the location of a battle between Britons and Saxons in 577: the traditionally accepted spot is Hinton Hill (Pathfinder 1167 741768), the site of a hill-fort, with the battle constituting an assault on the fort by either side. Information is limited to a short entry in the *Anglo-Saxon Chronicle*, to the effect that the Saxons Cuthwine and Ceawlin, killed three kings, Conmail, Condidan and Farinmail, thereby capturing Gloucester, Cirencester and Bath. Burne, in *More Battlefields of England*, suggests that the Britons took up a position along the present-day A46 (Pathfinder 1167 753770) and were gradually pushed back towards Hinton Hill by the advancing Saxon force which succeeded in outflanking them to the north and south. Whatever the nature of the action, the outcome split the West Country Britons into two separate communities based in Wales and Cornwall.

Any wider exploration of Lansdown will almost certainly include a visit to Bath (Landranger 172 7564). Held by Parliament during the opening months of the Civil War, it fell to the Royalists after Waller's dismal showing at Roundway Down and was not retaken until 30 July 1645. Waller's first wife, Jane, is buried in Bath Abbey (Pathfinder 1183 751648). Commissioned by Waller, her tomb lies in the north transept and includes effigies of both Jane and Waller himself. Perhaps, when his own time came, he had intended to be interred beside her. When the Royalist garrison moved in, troops defaced the monument and Waller, who married twice more, actually lies buried in the New Chapel, Westminster. The sufferings of Bath, and indeed, all garrison towns during the Civil War, regardless of which side had taken charge, are voiced by the mayor of the day: 'Our houses are emptied of all useful furniture . . . our poor suffer for want of victuals, and rich we have none.'

Although mortally wounded, Sir Bevil Grenville did not actually die on the battlefield at Lansdown, but in the sixteenth-century rectory in Cold Ashton (Pathfinder 1167 751727). The village lies off the A420, 1 mile from Marshfield (Pathfinder 1167 780737), the Royalist headquarters. The almshouses (Pathfinder 1167 774738) built in 1619 still preside over the western perimeter as they did in 1643 when witnessing the advances and withdrawals of the Royalist army.

Although the outskirts of Bristol (Landranger 172 5873) are only 3 miles from Lansdown, a foray into the urban sprawl will not yield much evidence of the importance of the city during the Civil War years: the castle and the seventeenth-century defences have all long since vanished. Standing by Christmas Steps is a modern plaque commemorating the death of Lieutenant-Colonel Henry Lunsford, a trusted aide of Prince Rupert, who was shot through the heart during the storming of the city after the Battle of Roundway Down.

In this part of the country, as a study of the pertinent Ordnance Survey maps will reveal, the tendency is for the explorer to be coaxed much further back in time. At Pucklechurch, for example, is to be found the supposed site of King Edmund's Palace (Pathfinder 1167 705765). Stanton Drew (Pathfinder 1183 601633) boasts one of the finest Neolithic religious sites in the country: three stone circles and a burial chamber. The Wansdyke (Pathfinder 1183 711630), running from Clevedon on the banks of the Severn to Inkpen Beacon near Hungerford (a distance of 80 miles) courses through the area; it may have been built in the fifth century as a defence by the Britons against the Saxons or by the Saxons themselves against invaders in the sixth century. It must have been an enormous undertaking, yet no mention of it is made in the *Anglo-Saxon Chronicle* which generally gives quite a full account of Saxon defences. According to rural tradition, it was built by the Devil on a Wednesday, hence the name.

Further Information

The hamlet of Lansdown lies 2 miles from the centre of Bath on the road to Wick. The battlefield of Lansdown is a further 2 miles from the hamlet. Motorists approaching the battlefield via the M4 should exit at Junction 18. Take the A46 Bath road past Dyrham Park. At the crossroads with the A420, turn right and then take the first left (Freezinghill Lane) which leads to the monument, where a little off-road parking is available.

Bath is well served by rail. For details of services between London (Paddington) and Bath Spa, telephone 0171 262 6767. For details of cross-country connections, telephone 01225 464446. Fortunately, the road to the battlefield services Bath Racecourse, so a connecting bus service is available. For details, telephone 01272 553231. Bath is also accessible by National Express coach. For details of cross-country services, telephone 0990 808080.

Further reading is readily available, accounts of the battle sometimes being paired with Roundway Down; for example, Robert Morris's booklet, *The Battles of Lansdown & Roundway*. An unusual, though welcome, addition to the Lansdown literature is Bob Moulder's comic strip *Western Wonders: The Battles of Lansdown and Roundway Down*. (Both these accounts are available via Caliver Books, 816–818 London Road, Leigh-on-Sea, Essex SS99 3NH, whose mail-order catalogue constitutes essential reading.) Much is known about both Lansdown and Roundway Down through the primary source material of Captain Richard Atkyns' memoirs, which make fascinating reading – see *The Vindication of Richard Atkyns* edited by Peter Young (Longman, 1967). In addition, accounts of Lansdown are to be found in Burne's *More Battlefields of England* and Rogers' *Battles and Generals of the Civil Wars*. Ordnance Survey maps of the area are Landranger 172 and Pathfinders 1183 and 1167, the latter Pathfinder sufficing at a pinch.

7
THE SIEGE OF GLOUCESTER
10 August–5 September 1643

Introduction

In AD 49 the Romans constructed a fortified harbour at Kingsholm to guard the lowest crossing point of the River Severn and to serve as a base for their invasion of Wales. Subsequently moved to the site of the present-day city centre, the fortress, known as Glevum, became the home of the 2nd Legion and achieved the status of *municipium*, one of only six in Britain. When the Romans departed, the settlement retained its significance by virtue of its position on the borders between Mercia and Wessex. Although Ethelreda, daughter of Alfred the Great, was responsible for extending the city, the long-term trend was for the country's power base to become established in the east, in London.

The Normans did not abandon Gloucester entirely, William the Conqueror continuing the tradition of holding annual councils there. At one such gathering in 1085 William set in motion plans for the Domesday survey. St Peter's Abbey, which later became Gloucester Cathedral, was also built at his instigation. In 1155 the city's status was recognized by Henry II, who conferred upon it a Royal charter and the nine-year-old Henry III was crowned here in 1216. During the Plantagenet period the great religious houses, the Franciscans, Dominicans, Carmelites and Augustinians (at Llanthony Priory), became established in Gloucester.

Religious matters also figured strongly in Tudor times, with St Peter's Abbey miraculously surviving the Dissolution to become a cathedral. In 1555, during the reign of 'Bloody Mary', the protestant Bishop Hooper was burnt at the stake in St Mary's Square.

By the mid-seventeenth century, Gloucester consisted of a medieval walled town surrounded by suburbs, and had a population of about 4,500. Although outshone by Bristol, the city's facilities as a port were being developed – Elizabeth I had granted Gloucester the status of a port in 1580,

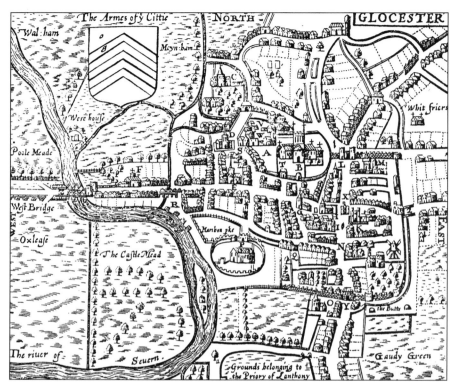

The City of Gloucester as depicted in John Speed's map of 1610. At the beginning of the siege, much of the housing which lay outside the city walls was fired by the garrison.

which allowed merchants to trade directly with foreign ports – and it seemed that nothing could stand in the way of further economic growth.

At the outbreak of the English Civil War, Gloucestershire came out largely in favour of Parliament. Taking a leading role in this respect, of course, were the Puritans. Despite its High Church associations, religious non-conformity had strong roots in Gloucester and was supported by the City Council. Archbishop Laud, champion of the established Church, had served as Dean of Gloucester from 1616 to 1621 and had become the focus of much local resentment at the time.

Naturally, there were many Royalist sympathizers among the landed gentry and, indeed, among the citizens of Gloucester, and each side in the conflict insisted that it could count upon the loyalty of the majority of the local people. However, certain of the king's actions had not endeared him to the 'floating voter'. For example, Gloucester clothiers were concerned at the increasing degree of central control to which the cloth industry was subject. Similarly, local tobacco growers were incensed at the Crown's attempts to abolish the industry in order to protect and encourage the new industries in the colony of Virginia. And Sir John Wyntour, the new owner of the Forest of Dean, had instituted a policy of enclosure which was not to the liking of the foresters. Doubtless, there were many more otherwise uncommitted groups who discovered that, for the time being at least, their best interests lay in supporting Parliament.

The Road to Gloucester

In charge of the Gloucester garrison was Lieutenant-Colonel Edward Massey, a professional soldier, only twenty-three years of age at the time of his appointment. On 2 February 1643, when Prince Rupert, having already taken Cirencester, made the first Royalist call for him to surrender, Massey replied that he had no intention of surrendering the city to a foreign prince.

Although the Siege of Gloucester proper did not commence until 10 August, freedom of movement to and from the city was becoming restricted as early as March, with Prince Maurice active to the north and east, and a Welsh army approaching from the west. Massey and Sir William Waller defused the situation by launching a successful coordinated assault on the Welsh but the respite proved to be only temporary, with Bristol's surrender to Prince Rupert on 26 July giving the Royalists an opportunity to turn on Gloucester with a vengeance.

The situation seemed hopeless. If Bristol could not hold out above three days, then what were Gloucester's chances of success? A specially convened Defence Committee took stock of the situation and expedited measures for patching up the dilapidated medieval town walls, largely through the construction of earthworks, which were much more effective against artillery than stone. Thus shovels and pickaxes became as much prized as swords and muskets. The walls, fronted in part by a ditch, had survived more or less intact to the east of the city from the South Gate to the North Gate. To the west, when the Westgate bridges were demolished, the River Severn provided a natural barrier. To the north, between the North Gate and the river, new earthworks had to be raised. The work was hard and tedious, and everyone, regardless of age, who was capable of wielding a spade was involved. Ditches had to be dug to a depth of 12 ft, and the earth thrown up to form a solid wall to the rear. Later, much was made of the cheery way everyone, including women and children, went about this work. However, it was compulsory, with the imposition of fines for slackers.

Despite the earthworks, the situation to the north might have been critical but for the marshy nature of the ground and the fact that it proved possible to flood some of it. To the south west, the construction of more earthworks, together with a half-moon bastion, were undertaken.

In addition to the extensive refurbishment programme, a number of outer defences were already in position. These included two sconces which had been constructed on Alney Island (the area of land enclosed by the River Severn to the west of the city) and a further one at The Vineyard, Over.

A curious omission in accounts of the siege defences is the role played by Gloucester Castle. A motte-and-bailey castle (covering a site defined by Commercial Road, Barbican Road and Ladybellegate Street) had been replaced during the twelfth century by a new structure further to the west, on a site now occupied by HM Prison. It played an active role in the Baron's War, and although it was reported to have fallen into disuse as early as the late fourteenth century, it continued to serve as a county gaol and was not finally demolished until the eighteenth century.

Fortunately for Gloucester's defenders, for whom time might otherwise have run out, the Royalist advance was gradual, with the establishment of main camps to the east of the city at Barton Hill; to the south east at Tredworth; to the west at Llanthony Priory; to the north west at Over, which the besieged had been forced to abandon; and to the north at Kingsholm, until at last the city found itself encircled by an army, the strength of which has been estimated as totalling 30,000 men.

The Siege of Gloucester

The Siege of Gloucester began on 10 August 1643 with an invitation for the city to surrender. A Royal pardon was promised to all the inhabitants, with a rider to the effect that should they refuse this generous offer, they must be prepared to suffer the consequences. A carefully worded reply assured the king that his dutiful subjects would hold Gloucester for him, obeying his commands as 'signified by both Houses of Parliament'. Throughout the war, Parliamentarians were always keen to stress their loyalty.

The Royalists immediately launched an assault from east and west, but the garrison set fire to the suburbs and the attack faltered. Massey also discovered that with a garrison of only 1,400, his resources were overstretched, so he abandoned his sconces on Alney Island and at The Vineyard. During the night, the Royalists cut the city's fresh water supply from the springs on Robinswood Hill.

With their overwhelming numerical superiority, the Royalists should have

The City of Gloucester from the lower reaches of Robinswood Hill.

been able to take the city with relative ease, but Charles seemed keen to starve the garrison into submission. Doubting the wisdom of this option, Prince Rupert, a man with little patience for prolonged sieges, would have preferred to leave Massey in situ. However, over the next few days, preparations were made for what was likely to be a long process. In particular, a bridge of boats was constructed and by 18 August, Colonel Sir William Vavasour was able to take his regiment across the River Severn and link up with the Worcester forces at Kingsholm.

In the meantime, the garrison had already embarked on the first of a series of plucky raids against the Royalist lines. As early as 11 August Captain-Lieutenant James Harcus led a raid on the Royalist trenches, acquiring for his pains an indeterminate number of shovels and pickaxes. Another raid on the following day won him more tools, with the addition of some guns and a few prisoners. On 15 August, during a third sally, he was killed.

These raids soon developed into something more than a nuisance for the Royalists. Their frequency alone rendered them an embarrassment, for while the besiegers were making such heavy work of trying to break in, the besieged apparently experienced no difficulty at all in breaking out. Particular attention was paid to the Kingsholm battery, with partially successful raids aimed at spiking the cannon made on 14 and 18 August. Not all raids were successful. One sally directed at Llanthony resulted in twenty-four Roundhead deaths. Probably the most ambitious Roundhead attack occurred on 21 August, when two separate parties sallied forth to attack the Royalists on both the south and east fronts, a bold enough plan which unfortunately foundered when the guide of one party lost his way.

Another characteristic of most prolonged sieges which occurred at Gloucester was mining on the part of the besiegers and counter-mining by the besieged. One tunnel, running towards the East Gate, was targeted by a garrison raiding party in the early hours of 1 September. In an action reminiscent of twentieth-century warfare, a hand-grenade was thrown into the tunnel, the surviving miners being shot down as they ran out. Attempts were also made to counter-mine the East Gate tunnel but, having been dug by professional miners from the Forest of Dean, it proved too deep. When the siege ended, the defenders were busy constructing 'great borers with which wee intended to bore through our mine into theirs, and so to drowne the enemie's mine'.

Curiously, civilians found it comparatively easy to come and go. With no line of circumnavigation, there were bound to be gaps in the defensive circle which might be exploited. Thus the defenders knew when help, in the shape of a relief column led by the Earl of Essex, was at hand. Less creditably, as far as the besiegers were concerned, cattle appear to have been turned out of the town to graze and hay was gathered in from Walham. In the light of such laxity on the part of the Royalists, it was perhaps inevitable that the city would be relieved. Food was never in short supply. In fact, the garrison claimed that it managed rather better than the Royalists in this respect. And so the besiegers were reduced to making empty threats to the effect that Essex had been defeated 'like a dog' – messages delivered with far less decorum than the king's original command.

Essex had left London on 26 August. As he approached, Charles, realizing that his plans had gone awry and not wishing to risk his cavalry in broken country, withdrew. On 4 September arrangements were made for the evacuation of the wounded and the following day, the Royalist army withdrew, allowing Essex, who arrived on 8 September after a slow march, to claim an easy victory.

The Aftermath

The tardy arrival of the Captain-General of the Parliamentary forces was attributed to the heavy cannon he insisted on taking with him. Perhaps he wished to avoid a confrontation with an army nearly double the size of his own – although he could have counted upon Massey's full support. As they approached the city, its suburbs gutted by fire, the troops of the rambling relief column may have received the impression that conditions were as bad as had been expected. An additional 5,000 men had been recruited, the capital's shops having been closed so as to give the 'nation of shop-keepers' an opportunity to fight for their country, if not for their king.

Once inside the walls, however, the new militia may have noted that the populace displayed few signs of under-nourishment. Casualties had been very light. Both sides, in the propaganda war, had wildly overestimated the number of enemy dead. The garrison dead could be counted in tens rather than in hundreds. The Royalists, who admitted to having lost a hundred dead, may have lost many more, yet, undoubtedly, Massey's response from within was far superior to the management of operations from without.

Tales of rape and pillage committed by the Royalist rank and file began to filter in from the surrounding countryside – which must be balanced with stories of the unruly behaviour of Massey's troops. The arrival of Essex's 15,000 troops would have amounted, therefore, to something of a mixed blessing as far as the civilians were concerned. With an estimated 241 houses destroyed by fire, overcrowding within the walls was rife. No one knew how long the war would last, and work could not begin on rebuilding for fear of another siege occurring in the future. If nothing else, the siege had drawn attention to the relatively poor state of the city defences and considerable repair work was put in hand.

Such repairs as were made must have been minimal for by 1650, when the future Charles II launched his premature bid for power, the defences were once again described as 'ruinous'. With Charles's arrival at Worcester, it seemed that Gloucester was again under potential threat, necessitating the creation, once more, of a garrison of 1,400 men. Prior to the Battle of Worcester, the citizens of Gloucester sent ammunition and supplies to the Roundhead army. After his victory at Worcester, Cromwell accepted the honour of becoming High Steward of the city.

As soon as the crisis had passed, the defences were allowed to deteriorate again and moves were made to dispense with the garrison. However, with both real and imagined Royalist plots continuing to unsettle Parliament throughout the 1650s, Gloucester, along with many other cities, remained on the alert. As late as 1657, concern was being expressed about the decay of the city walls.

At the Restoration, the Gloucestershire Royalist gentry recovered much of their former influence at the expense of the merchant class. Perhaps the most unusual case of 'rehabilitation' was that of Massey himself, who was elected MP for Gloucester in 1661. Following particularly shabby treatment by the Parliament he had served so well, he became a committed Royalist, using his influence in the city to aid the Stuart cause.

Economically, it is debatable as to how much long-term damage Gloucester suffered as a direct result of the siege. In the short term, the city was driven to the verge of bankruptcy. From its own resources it was expected to purchase arms and ammunition and to shoulder the cost of fortifications. In addition, the troops constituting the garrison had to be lodged, fed and paid – a burden which continued throughout the war, although to a lesser extent as Parliament became able to offer more direct assistance. Recovery did not truly begin until the eighteenth century when the suburbs were rebuilt and traditional industries began to flourish once more.

The Walk

Distance: 6 miles (9.7 km)

Begin at the Tourist Information Centre beneath St Michael's Tower at The Cross (Pathfinder 1089 832186) (Point A). Walk up Westgate Street. On the right-hand side of the road, look out for No. 30 (Euroglaze office). At the time of the siege, it was occupied by an apothecary, James Commeline, whose services must have been much in demand. On 25 August 1643 a red-hot cannonball – an incendiary device – careered through three houses and came to rest in No. 30; it was cooled only with the greatest difficulty.

A little further along, on the right, College Street leads to Gloucester Cathedral. In particular, look out for the east window, dating from 1349, which commemorates the contribution of local gentry to the victory at Crècy (1346) and the Siege of Calais (1347). The cathedral appears to have come through the siege comparatively unscathed, though some of the stained glass sustained damage at the hands of the Earl of Leven's army as it passed through Gloucester in 1645. The effigy in the South Ambulatory of Robert, Duke of Normandy, eldest son of William the Conqueror, who died in 1134, was also defaced at this time. There are also two other monuments with a Civil War connection – those of Thomas Fitzwilliams and William White. The latter, who served with Massey during the siege, was killed at Raglan Castle in 1646.

Return to Westgate Street. On the left, at the corner of Upper Quay Street, is the Crown Inn, Massey's headquarters. Royalist artillery scored at least one direct hit on the building when a cannonball 'of about twenty pound in weight' burst in. Further along, occupying 99–103 Westgate Street, is the Gloucester Folk Museum, which contains displays of Civil War interest – and holds a key for visitors to the redundant Church of St Nicholas across the road. The spire has a truncated appearance because Royalist guns destroyed the top half: its restoration was not a long-term success, and the structure had to be shortened.

Continue along Westgate Street and turn left into The Quay. The medieval castle once stood on the land to the right, stretching down to Commercial Street. Bear right into Severn Road and carry on into

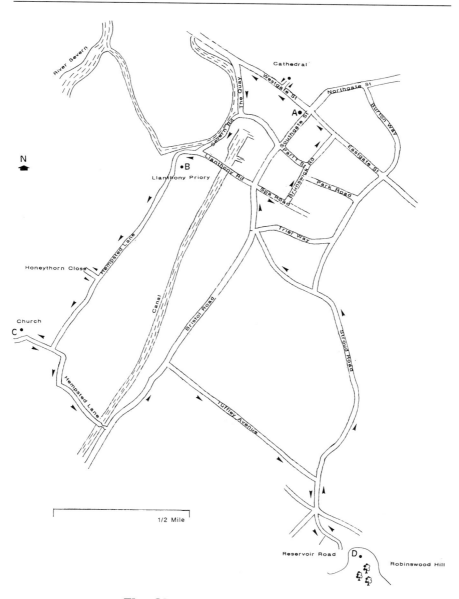

The Siege of Gloucester, 1643

Llanthony Road, and the remains of Llanthony Priory (Pathfinder 1089 824180) (Point B), currently (1995) undergoing restoration by English Heritage. Llanthony Road develops into Hempsted Lane. A short detour up Honeythorne Close (Pathfinder 1089 818174) leads to the remains of the Royalist earthworks at Newark. At the end of Hempsted Lane a right turn into St Swithun's Road brings one to Hempsted churchyard (Pathfinder 1089 814170) (Point C) and the well preserved tomb of John Freeman, a Royalist officer killed during the siege.

Returning from the churchyard, carry straight on down St Swithun's Road and (with care) negotiate the narrow Hempsted Bridge to emerge on to Bristol Road. Turn left and then right at the traffic lights into Tuffley Avenue, lined with Victorian and Edwardian villas. At the end, turn right into Stroud Road and walk down to the roundabout. Follow the sign to Robinswood Hill Country Park, the entrance to which (Pathfinder 1089 837158) (Point D) is on Reservoir Road.

One could easily spend a pleasant afternoon here. A network of footpaths enables one to see the wells which supplied Gloucester with water, and which the Royalists were quick to cut. Charles I stayed at Matson House (Pathfinder 1089 848156) on the western edge of the hill. The view over Gloucester from the lower slopes is extensive; from the summit, it is magnificent.

Return to the roundabout and follow Stroud Road into the centre of Gloucester. However, instead of continuing into Southgate, turn right into Spa Road and then left into Brunswick Road. The Royalist battery on Gaudy Green (bordered by Brunswick Square) on the left, was uncomfortably close to the city defences, the south-west corner of which can be identified by the curve of Brunswick Road and Parliament Street.

At the top of Brunswick Street, turn into Eastgate Street. On the left, in front of Boots, is a curious glass structure, which turns out to be a splendid viewing chamber for the remains of the East Gate, excavated in 1974. Continue on to The Cross and the starting point, choosing any one of the city centre's excellent public houses at which to take refreshment.

Further Explorations

On the outskirts of Gloucester, at Over, on the site of the palace of the Bishop of Gloucester, may be seen the defensive earthworks thrown up by the besieged and later taken over by the Royalists (Pathfinder 1089 814198).

Cheltenham, directly to the east of Gloucester, is something of a disappointment because at the time of the Civil War it was a village of little value to the military, apart from being used as a Royalist base during the siege. However, 11 miles farther on is Winchcombe and Sudeley Castle (Landranger 163 0627), home of Lord Chandos. Only temporarily held for Parliament early in 1643, Sudeley remained a Royalist base until June 1644 when it was taken by Waller. Interior panelling was used for firewood and the tomb of Catherine Parr – Henry VIII's sixth wife had been buried in the chapel in 1548 – was desecrated. Slighted in 1649, the castle has since undergone considerable restoration.

Painswick, 6 miles south of Gloucester (Landranger 162 8609) was a Royalist base, the king lodging here in Court House on 10 August 1643. Roundhead prisoners were held in St Mary's Church. One such prisoner, Richard Foot, indulged in a little stone carving: 'Be bold, be bold, but not too bold.' Along with Foot's graffiti, the damage wreaked by artillery fire on the church tower can still be seen. Another vandalized tomb belongs to Sir Anthony Kingston, friend of Henry VIII. Much hated by local people because of his enthusiasm in suppressing opposition to the Dissolution of the Monasteries, memory of him remained sufficiently strong for folk to desecrate his tomb under cover of St Mary's bombardment.

In March 1643 at Highnam, 3 miles to the north east (Landranger 162 7919), Lord Herbert's Welsh Royalists – 2,000 strong – took possession of Sir Robert Cooke's manor house. Hastily thrown up defensive earthworks survive in the vicinity of the churchyard. A Roundhead force led by Waller and Sir Edward Massey attacked the stronghold on 24 March, forcing the surrender of most of Herbert's men. A number who succeeded in breaking out were caught and cut down at Barber's Bridge, near Tibberton (Landranger 162 7722). A monument marks the spot where eighty-six bodies were uncovered during the nineteenth century.

A little to the north of Tibberton is Taynton (Landranger 162 7372), of interest because of its church. The village was the scene of some heavy fighting, during the course of which the medieval church was destroyed; it was replaced by the present traditionally simplistic Puritan structure. The churchyard contains a monument to Thomas Pury, MP for Gloucester, who fought in the Town Regiment during the siege.

Haresfield Hill, 5 miles to the south (Landranger 162 8209), an excellent viewing point, was probably recognized as such by the Royalists during the siege. Indeed the summit has a siege memorial, occasionally (and misleadingly) referred to as the 'Cromwell Stone'. Other locations associated with Cromwell are Chavenage House (Landranger 162 8795) near Tetbury, allegedly visited by both Cromwell and Ireton in 1648 in order to canvass the owner for his support in putting the king on trial. The chambers in which they were supposedly lodged are known as the Cromwell and Ireton rooms. A further unsubstantiated claim relates to Cromwell having lodged at Cromwell House in the village of Naunton (Landranger 163 1123). The house, owned by the Aylworth family, was named in Cromwell's honour. St Andrew's Church contains a memorial to one Ambrose Oldys, a Royalist, inscribed to the effect that he was 'barbarously murdered by ye rebells' – demonstrating that the conflict could wreak deep divisions in the smallest of communities.

Further Information

Motorists may approach Gloucester via Junction 11 of the M5 or across country via the A40. Long-stay parking facilities are currently (1995) available at several sites in the town centre for a reasonable £1.50. Weekday visits present no problems, but Saturdays are best avoided, congestion having led to the introduction of a Park and Ride scheme.

Rail travellers can use the through-service between London (Paddington) and Gloucester (telephone 0171262 6767 for information). For details of cross-country rail services, telephone 01452 529501. For details of National Express coach services between London (Victoria) and Gloucester, and of services linking Gloucester with other parts of the country, telephone 0990 808080.

Further reading is provided by the excellent *Gloucester and the Civil War: A City Under Siege* by Malcolm Atkin and Wayne Laughlin, while Peter Young's *Sieges of the Great Civil War* includes an appropriate chapter. The locally published *Historic Gloucester* by Philip Moss is also available. Ordnance Survey maps covering Gloucester are Landranger 162 and Pathfinder 1089. As with all town walks, the purchase of a street map is advisable.

The Tourist Information Office (which holds very little information about Civil War Gloucester) is situated at The Cross (telephone 01452 421188). Gloucester's bookshops are also reticent on the subject. The best source is the Folk Museum (open Monday–Saturday 10.00–17.00 and Sunday 10.00–16.00 from July to September only) which can be visited as part of the suggested walk.

The problem with planning a Civil War walk in Gloucester is that there is so much of unrelated interest which is likely to attract one's attention en route. For example, several museums, including the Regiments of Gloucester Museum, are housed in The Docks development. Although the renovated designer warehousing is not to everyone's taste, the complex (fronted by the Mariners' Chapel) represents a real effort to adapt the architecture of the nineteenth century to the social and economic needs of the twentieth. Once one has begun to explore Gloucester, it is difficult to know where to stop, and a visit of at the very least a weekend's duration is recommended.

8
THE FIRST BATTLE OF NEWBURY
20 September 1643

Introduction

The Siege of Gloucester and the Battle of Newbury must be seen as part of a single campaign, for the lifting of the siege led directly to the battle fought two weeks later. Because of this, the two events are often described together but, although there must be some overlap, for the purposes of this volume – and for greater clarity – they are considered separately.

As far as the Earl of Essex was concerned, the Newbury campaign began with plans for Gloucester's relief. As already noted, there was great concern in the capital over Gloucester's ultimate fate. The decision to send a relief force, which owed much to the encouragement of John Pym, placed Essex in a difficult position. Waller's name had been mentioned during discussions about a possible leader, but Essex, viewing the expedition as an opportunity to enhance his own professional standing, decided to take charge personally, leaving Waller to safeguard the capital. It became necessary to recruit afresh owing to sickness among the Roundhead troops. A few weeks before Essex's departure, his officers claimed that half of his foot soldiers were ill, a problem caused by 'want of pay' and poor clothing. Conditions were not much improved by the date of the relief force's departure, with its soldiers, despite having received two weeks' pay, still very much in arrears.

Essex left Colnbrook, near Slough, on 27 August 1643, for Beaconsfield, from where he moved on to Bierton, near Aylesbury, where, according to contemporary reports, his army was clothed. Thus, two of his officers' major complaints had been partially addressed. A few miles further on, Sir Philip Stapleton's force, quartered at Grendon Underwood (the main body being a little to the rear at Waddesdon) took on 400 Royalist horse at Bicester. The Cavaliers were soon put to flight, being pursued through and beyond Bicester for a distance of some 2 miles.

On 1 September Essex reached Brackley, a rendezvous point where he was joined by additional troops. He set up his headquarters at Aynho, while his Lieutenant-General of Horse, Colonel John Middleton, was posted to Deddington. Hearing that two regiments of Royalist horse were in possession of the town, a party of horse and dragoons was ordered to advance. At their approach, the Royalists withdrew towards Oxford. In pursuit, the Roundhead force came upon the enemy, reinforced by fifty troopers commanded by Lord Wilmot. The next day, some fighting between these opposing forces took place. Although described as a skirmish rather than a battle, the action continued from morning until three o'clock in the afternoon. The Roundheads, under Middleton and Sir James Ramsay, ended the day by being chased back into Deddington, the pursuing party of Royalist horse being beaten back upon reaching the town.

On 3 September Essex covered the 12 miles to Chipping Norton, where more Royalist horse were brushed aside, and then moved on to Stow-on-the-Wold, where he found Prince Rupert, with 4,000 horse, awaiting him. The prince lost no time in dispatching a strong party of cavalry to assault the Roundhead column. Although they were beaten back, a Roundhead forlorn hope commanded by a Captain Carr was cut off from his own lines, a predicament from which he was extricated by the efforts of a body of musketeers who drove off the Royalist horse.

Rupert now drew off, only to reappear 3 miles further on. For a second time, he was forced to withdraw, although he continued to shadow Essex for the rest of the day – 4 September – until Essex pitched camp at Naunton, 10 miles east of Cheltenham. Much was made of the gallantry of the Roundhead officers in holding Rupert at bay, but one suspects that the 40 pieces of artillery which Essex had insisted on taking with him had some bearing on the situation.

The next day, Essex reached Prestbury, still 10 miles short of Gloucester, and fired salvoes from four of his great guns on Prestbury Hill, thereby giving the king notice of his arrival. And there, by Prestbury Hill, the Roundheads spent a wretched night in the rain, cold and half-starved; a night, one imagines, far worse than that endured by the Gloucester garrison to whose relief it had marched.

The Road to Newbury

In some respects, when he learned of the withdrawal of the besieging force, Essex must have experienced a sense of anticlimax. His march had been long and tedious, and fraught with danger. Always fearing that he might be outflanked, worried about the possibility that he would fall victim to a night assault by Royalist cavalry, he arrived at journey's end to find the bird flown.

After a few skirmishes at Cheltenham, where he passed two nights, Essex moved on to Gloucester, spending the weekend of 8–10 September in the city. He was able to provide the garrison with ammunition and money, but nothing in the way of food because none was to be had, the Royalists having destroyed all about them. Therefore, on 10 September the relief army marched to Tewkesbury, to provide cover for revictualling expeditions into Herefordshire.

Finally, on Friday 15 September, Essex turned about to commence what he hoped would be a relatively swift return to London. Originally he had intended to march as far as Cheltenham on the first day but, on receiving intelligence that some of Prince Maurice's men were in Cirencester with provisions for the Royalist army, he resolved to launch a surprise attack. At 1.00 a.m. the next morning, the Royalists were taken unawares by the vanguard of the Roundhead army, led by Essex himself. The result was a haul of several hundred prisoners and forty wagons of supplies – of which Essex was by now in dire need.

It seemed that the tide of events was now turning in Parliament's favour, and it has been argued that the Siege of Gloucester constituted the watershed. Charles may have realized this, for he had abandoned the siege in a dejected frame of mind. En route to Newbury, his younger son, the Duke of York, asked him whether they were now going home. Sitting down wearily on a milestone, the king replied, 'We have no home.'

Since leaving Essex in possession of Gloucester, Charles had been following at a safe distance, always staying marginally out of reach. With Essex at Gloucester, the Royalists had camped at Sudeley Castle. When Essex had marched to Tewkesbury, Charles had followed suit to Evesham. A Roundhead move towards Upton-upon-Severn had been countered by a Royalist march to Worcester. Clearly the king's plan was to keep his own army always between Essex and London. Hoping to get home by taking a more southerly route, Essex made forced marches to Cricklade and Swindon, aiming to reach Hungerford by the evening of 18 September. The Royalists were still to the east, having progressed via Stow-on-the-Wold, Burford and Lechlade.

Realizing that Essex was within a whisker of being home and dry, Prince Rupert, at the head of an estimated 5,000–6,000 cavalry, pressed on, intercepting the Roundhead rearguard 6 miles to the north of Hungerford, at Aldbourne. The Roundhead cavalry was thrown back, in confusion, on to the infantry. Having managed to regroup, with a view to covering the infantry withdrawal, they were put to flight a second time. There followed charge and spirited counter-charge, but Rupert lacked the strength to drive home his advantage, and towards evening he was forced to break off the engagement.

But he had succeeded in slowing down Essex's progress, and while the

Roundheads were recovering in Hungerford, Charles managed to reach Newbury ahead of them. In fact the Royalist march was so swift that 1,500 infantrymen failed to reach the battlefield in time to fight. On 19 September, when Essex was within 2 miles of Newbury, he realized that the king had taken possession of the town and that a battle was now inevitable – as was another miserable night without shelter for the Roundhead army. Essex veered to the south, away from the present-day A4, via the village of Hamstead Marshall, to bivouac in the fields to the south west of Newbury. And the Royalists, it appeared, had even taken possession of the one topographical feature which would prove to be of vital strategic importance in any battle – Round Hill.

The First Battle of Newbury

Early on the morning of 20 September 1643 the Earl of Essex deployed his men over Wash Common. He had expected to see the Royalists in possession of Round Hill, but it turned out that the cavalry espied on it the previous evening was only a reconnaissance party. Essex originally intended to divide the Roundhead army into two wings, with Skippon taking command of the left wing, while Essex assumed personal command of the right wing. However, the Royalist line was much longer than Essex had anticipated and he found it necessary to extend his own line to the Newbury–Kintbury road. Thus the Roundheads now had a left wing of infantry (Major Richard Fortescue and Colonel Lord Robartes) and cavalry (Colonel John Middleton). Their right wing comprised cavalry (Lieutenant-General Sir Philip Stapleton), with the infantry of Essex and Skippon in the centre, manoeuvring into position on Round Hill.

The Royalists (with the king himself in command) now had to take Round Hill, which was clearly the key to the battle and which could have been occupied with ease the night before. The Royalist left wing comprised the cavalry of Prince Rupert and Colonel Charles Gerrard. Infantry commanded by Colonel Sir William Vavasour filled the right, with more infantry commanded by Colonel Sir Nicholas Byron and the cavalry of Colonel John Byron and Colonel Sir Arthur Ashton in the centre. The battle opened with an assault on Round Hill by Sir Nicholas Byron and Sir John Byron (uncle and nephew respectively). With artillery on the plateau and good cover afforded by hedgerows, the defenders were well placed. None the less, although suffering heavy casualties, the Byrons managed to establish a foothold on the north-east corner.

Contemporary accounts of the action on the Roundhead left are scant, but Fortescue did initially come under intense pressure from Vavasour. With the baggage train to his rear, it was essential that Fortescue held on, and it became necessary for him to be reinforced by Colonel Sir William Springate's regiment.

On the Roundhead right wing, over ground more suitable for cavalry than the centre, Rupert launched one of his famous charges against Stapleton. It took three assaults to make Stapleton give ground. When he did so, the Royalist cavalry over played its hand by pushing too far forward. Although many were ambushed by dragoons sheltering behind the hedges to the rear, Stapleton's cavalry had been broken. Essex was to be found in among the fleeing cavalry, trying to rally them, leaving Skippon to direct operations.

The turning point in the battle occurred when Skippon ordered more artillery forward to engage the Royalist guns based near the tumuli on Wash Common. He also brought up his remaining reserves, the London Trained Bands of Lieutenant-Colonel Tucker and Lieutenant-Colonel West, and sent one of the two remaining auxiliary regiments to support Essex.

Although now stable, the Roundhead centre was still suffering from the Royalist artillery. According to one account, a Royalist officer, Captain John Gwynne, saw a file of Roundhead infantry, six deep, with their heads struck off by a single cannon shot, but the pike-men stood firm, repulsing a further charge from Rupert. And the Roundhead demiculverins, in turn, wrought considerable havoc among the Royalist cavalry and foot.

The armies had been hotly engaged throughout the entire day and neither side, through exhaustion, could make any headway. With the onset of darkness, the firing of the guns became sporadic as both Roundheads and Royalists withdrew to their original positions.

The Aftermath

When the fighting drew to a close towards 7.00 p.m. the Roundheads could have been forgiven for thinking that hostilities would be resumed at daybreak. Although both sides had suffered heavy casualties, the Royalists had lost many men of rank, including Secretary of State, Lord Falkland, and the gallant Earl of Carnarvon who had distinguished himself at Lansdown earlier in the year (see p 66–7). The main problem for the Royalists, however, was the fact that they were running short of ammunition, Sir Henry Percy reporting that only ten barrels of powder remained from the ninety barrels with which they had begun the day. Rupert, all for holding on until the expected fresh supplies arrived, was overruled by the king, who ordered a withdrawal to Oxford.

Lucius Cary, Viscount Falkland, one of the king's two secretaries of state. It is a commonly held belief that Falkland, depressed and overworked, committed suicide by spurring his horse into a reckless charge. Perhaps he experienced a presentiment of his death. In any event, he had prepared for it by donning clean underwear on the morning of the battle. (Mansell Collection)

The Roundheads, meanwhile, were being encouraged by their commanders to return to the fray the following day and it must have come as a welcome surprise indeed on the morning of 21 September to discover the road to the capital open. Their homeward march was not to prove uneventful for Rupert had won permission to follow and harass the rearguard. Near Aldermaston, the prince caught Stapleton's cavalry unawares in a narrow country lane and created much disorder before being beaten off by concentrated musket fire. On 28 September Essex arrived in London to receive a hero's welcome.

In terms of casualties, Newbury must be seen as a drawn contest. In total, about 3,500 men, made up of roughly an equal number on both sides, lost their lives. Both commanders appeared to be solicitous about care of the dead and wounded, Essex instructing the parish constables of Enburn to attend to the burial of all corpses, while the king ordered the Mayor of Newbury to ensure that all wounded Roundheads were to receive the same medical care as the Royalists. As it was usual for the victorious general to give permission for enemy wounded to be carried away, perhaps Charles used the custom as a means of claiming a victory.

In retrospect, however, the Roundheads must be regarded as the winners, if only because Essex had achieved his purpose of marching to Gloucester, raising the siege and marching back again. Charles, on the other hand, had failed in his objective of cornering Essex and destroying his army. For the moment, therefore, Essex was the Parliamentarian man of the moment. Ironically, it was in part the Roundheads' failure at the Second Battle of Newbury one year later that led to his downfall.

In the long term, the First Battle of Newbury had unfortunate results for the Royalist command and, in particular, Prince Rupert for, with the death of Lord Falkland, it became necessary to appoint another Secretary of State. The job went to Lord Digby, the man who had once aroused Rupert from his sickbed to ask him to find some petards (mines) because he had no idea what they were. The prince's indifference to Digby was balanced by the new secretary's ambition, which he saw could be furthered by exploiting the growing rift between Rupert and Queen Henrietta. The courtly intrigue which had always been a feature of campaign discussions in the Royalist camp thus took on a new lease of life.

It has been said that the Newbury campaign was the Royalists' last chance to win the war. Prospects for their main hope of success – the delivery of an early knockout blow – were beginning to fade, and as time wore on, so the likelihood of a Parliamentary victory would increase. Ominously, it had been a shortage of ammunition which had led to the Royalist withdrawal, and shortages could grow only more acute as Parliament exploited its hold on the country's chief seaports and its influence in the major manufacturing areas.

The Walk

Distance: 7 miles (11.27 km)

Begin at the railway station in Newbury (Pathfinder 1187 472667) (Point A). Walk up Station Road in a westerly direction, cross Bartholomew Street and continue up Pound Street into Enborne Road which defines the northernmost limits of the action. The end of the built-up area is defined by Enborne Gate Farm (Pathfinder 1187 458664), which may also be identified as the northernmost Royalist position occupied by Vavasour. Continue to Skinners Green Lane and turn left towards Skinners Green. This area, occupied by Fortescue, Middleton and Robartes witnessed heavy fighting.

Walk on to Skinners Green, then bear left into Cope Hall Lane, leading up to Round Hill (Pathfinder 1187 452651) (Point B), the important position smartly occupied by Skippon's brigade and, at the time of the battle, peppered with enclosures. At the junction, bear right into Enborne

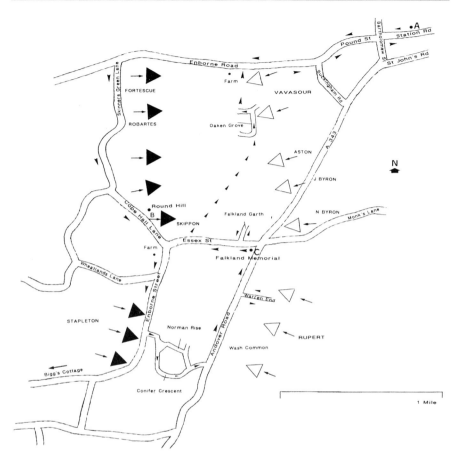

The First Battle of Newbury, 1643

Street. Wash Common Farm (Pathfinder 1187 452649) on the right was, again, the scene of some of the heaviest fighting.

The site occupied by Stapleton on the southern Roundhead flank is unclear. Some authorities suggest a site towards the end of the modern housing estate while others suggest that the Roundhead line stretched as far as the River Enborne. Either way, the battle was fought along a very wide front. Cut through the housing estate via Conifer Crescent (Pathfinder 1187 451643) to join Andover Road and walk back towards Newbury.

Newbury is not among the most haunted of Civil War battlefields. However, by taking an optional detour along Enborne Street for ¾ mile, one arrives at the privately owned Bigg's Cottage (Pathfinder 1187 438637),

The Falkland Memorial, Newbury. Barrett's
Battles and Battlefields in England, published
in 1896, contains a sketch of the memorial in
open countryside. Today the area is
thoroughly urbanized, with the memorial not
visible until one is almost upon it.

where Essex reputedly spent the night before the battle. In his *Battles and Generals of the Civil Wars*, Colonel Rogers recalls speaking to one of the owners who reported a sighting in her bedroom of 'a short man . . . wearing a maroon coloured coat', whom she identified as the earl.

Returning to Andover Road, cross over to the right-hand side and continue to the track, Warren End (Pathfinder 1187 458647), leading to the school, beyond which the lands opens out on to what little remains of Wash Common and the position occupied by Prince Rupert. After viewing, turn back and continue along Andover Road to the Falkland Memorial (Pathfinder 1187 460650) (Point C), where Falkland met his death and behind which, at the junction with Essex Street, lies the aptly named Gun Inn, supposedly the king's headquarters during the battle, at which refreshment may be taken.

Emerging from the inn, turn right into Essex Street. According to legend, Lord Falkland's body was brought for burial to Falkland Farm, now Falkland Garth (Pathfinder 1187 458650). Near the end of Essex Street there is a post office and general stores and, opposite, a public footpath (Pathfinder 1187 455651) following the perimeter of another housing estate. Take this path and walk in a north-easterly direction towards the starting point. The vista to the left soon opens out to reveal the slopes of Round Hill. Running between the field and the hedge bordering the housing development, the path is overgrown in places and a secondary path (not a right of way) appears to have developed in the field alongside. At the school, a stile has to be negotiated and one walks into Oaken Grove to pick up the path leading through the trees to Enborne Gate Farm. At the farm, turn right into Enborne Road and walk back to the railway station. A short walk into the town centre will take one to the museum, the Jacobean Old Cloth Hall, in Wharf Street (Pathfinder 1187 473672) which contains artefacts from the battlefield and offers an audio-visual presentation of both the First and Second Battles of Newbury.

Further Explorations

In the course of a visit to the site of the First Battle of Newbury, it would seem negligent to ignore the site of the Second Battle of Newbury which took place on 27 October 1644. Although much of the battlefield has suffered from urban development and lacks the potential for a comprehensive circular walk, it is not without its points of interest.

Both Royalists and Roundheads were actively seeking a fight, the former to avenge their defeat on Marston Moor, the latter (in the person of Essex) to restore a reputation sorely dented by the failure of his Lostwithiel campaign.

The king's initial objective of raising the siege of Donnington Castle quickly developed into a battle for survival when the Royalist army of 10,000 men found itself boxed in to the north of old Newbury by the three Roundhead armies of Essex, Manchester and Waller, the latter having successfully completed a 13 mile outflanking manoeuvre. The Royalist positions were bounded by Speen village and the present-day Shaw House. Threatening Prince Maurice at Speen were Waller, with Skippon and Cromwell, while at Shaw House, Lieutenant-Colonel Lisle faced Manchester. At about 3.00 p.m. on 27 October, Waller launched an attack on Prince Maurice's positions, forcing the Royalists back towards Newbury. A counter-charge directed by Goring saved the day and Cromwell, making his customary late appearance to clear the table and take the credit, was forced to retreat in some disorder. On the eastern side of the town, Manchester, seemingly unaware of Waller's assault, finally attacked Shaw House at around 4.00 p.m. but was himself driven back. As darkness fell, bringing the fighting to a close, both sides thought they were beaten. Charles, therefore, contrived to withdraw to Oxford during the night while Manchester, concerned over the vulnerability of his own position, took no precautions to stop him.

The high ground of Clay Hill (Pathfinder 1187 485683) where Manchester deployed his troops is still open land. At the time of the battle, the Elizabethan manor, Shaw House, in Love Lane (Pathfinder 1187 475684) was known as Dolemans, and lent itself admirably to fortification, the hedges and hollows of its extensive grounds providing excellent cover for marksmen. The fourteenth-century Donnington Castle (Pathfinder 1187 461692) was held by the Royalists throughout the Civil War, surviving numerous attacks and sieges. Following the Second Battle of Newbury, Waller renewed the siege but was forced to retire at the approach of another relief force. When the time to surrender finally came in 1646, the castle suffered the sad fate of many another ancient pile when it was razed to the ground. Waller's battle positions (Pathfinder 1187 454691 to 1187 448681) to the west of Speen between the River Lambourne and the Bath road (the present-day A4) have, like Manchester's, retained an open aspect. Waller's outflanking march took him via Hermitage, Chieveley, Winterbourne, Boxford and present-day Stockcross. It is said that Cromwell lodged at the Blue Boar Inn near Chieveley (Landranger 174 4773) on the night before the battle.

Another Berkshire town which should have some interest for students of the Civil War is Reading (Landranger 175 7173) which changed hands several times between 1642 and 1645. Once again, however, urbanization has destroyed much of value, although remains of a redoubt constructed by the Royalists may be viewed in Forbury Gardens. At the conclusion of a twelve-day siege in April 1643, Colonel Richard Fielding surrendered to Essex. Court-martialled for his action and sentenced to death, he was reprieved through Prince Rupert's intercession with the king. Fielding, who had fought at Edgehill, and continued to fight as a volunteer after the Siege of Reading, had negotiated the surrender on behalf of the wounded governor, Sir Arthur Aston, whose injuries conveniently prohibited speech.

Further Information

Newbury is situated on the A34, midway between Oxford and Winchester. The M4 crosses the A34 just 4 miles to the north of the town. Car parking, much of it short term, is available in the town centre. Motorists who gravitate towards the Kennet Centre multi-storey car park should note that the upper levels only relate to long-term parking. Early arrivals may be fortunate enough to secure space on the Newbury railway station car park – the starting point for the walk.

Newbury's traffic problems are well known, with A34 southbound queues for the town centre stretching back beyond the M4 junction. Hence, if possible, it is a good idea to make one's journey by rail. Newbury is on the Inter-City London–Penzance line, with a through journey from London (Paddington) to Newbury taking forty-five minutes; telephone 0171 387 7070 for further details. A National Express coach option is also available via the Oxford–Bournemouth route; telephone 0990 808080.

Accounts of the battle are to be found in Young and Adair's *From Hastings to Culloden*, Seymour's *Battles in Britain 1642–1746* and Colonel H.C.B. Rogers' *Battles and Generals of the Civil Wars*. In addition, the specialist Partizan Press have published a valuable booklet: *The Forlorn Hope Guide to the First Battle of Newbury* by David Frampton and Peter Garnham. Ordnance Survey maps of the area are Landranger 174 and Pathfinder 1187.

First Newbury (as the battle is known in professional circles) has been the subject of some controversy because of the planned western by-pass. At the time of writing (1995) permission for the scheme has been granted, although the new battle for the preservation of the battlefield itself is far from over. The proposed road will follow the course of the old Didcot, Newbury and Southampton railway line (Pathfinder 1187 448660), to the west of the field of battle. Critics are alarmed at the resulting opportunities for the creation of housing developments and factory estates on the land between the by-pass and the present western perimeter of urban Newbury, although not all local inhabitants agree, as one will discover when talking to people – an essential and rewarding activity in all battlefield walks – who live and work in the immediate area.

It is unlikely that the by-pass will be stopped, and motorists will appreciate that the town is in dire need of the relief it will provide. Protesters would be well advised, therefore, to heed the lesson of Naseby, where the campaign in respect of the A14 gave some priority to ensuring that access to the battlefield site was unimpeded, with a consequent extension of the planned access road system.

9
THE BATTLE OF CHERITON
29 March 1644

Introduction

Following the Lansdown–Roundway Down campaign, an uncharacteristically grateful king had created Hopton 'Lord Hopton of Stratton' and placed him in command of a new army, with a semi-roving commission to secure Dorset, Wiltshire and Hampshire. Things had not gone so well for Hopton's friend, Waller, who had also entertained hopes of a promotion. Despite opposition from Essex, John Pym had assured Waller of his support. Unfortunately, Pym died before that promise bore fruit, adding further fuel to Waller's reputation as an 'unlucky' general.

At that time, Parliament was divided between those – including Essex – whose thoughts were turning to a negotiated peace settlement and others who preferred to fight to the finish. The latter party voiced the idea of a 'New Army', staffed by staunch Puritans and led by Waller. Although his own religious convictions were well known, Waller could not bring himself to support a move which paid scant regard to a prospective officer's military ability. And so, having fallen out with both his enemies and his friends, his position remained uncertain. Not until January 1644 was he confirmed as commander of the Southern Association – the forces raised in Hampshire, Surrey, Sussex and Kent – and he was compelled to embark on operations in the autumn of 1643 without the authority he needed.

The Royalists commenced their campaign in October 1642 by seizing Winchester. Waller set out from London with the intention of taking it back, but instead turned his attention to Basing House. After a futile siege lasting nine days (see pp 108–9), he fell back on Basingstoke before establishing winter quarters at Farnham, blaming the unreliability of the London Trained Bands for his lack of progress. It was felt by his critics that Waller should have advanced on Hopton's army which had been within 2 miles of Basingstoke immediately before his withdrawal to Farnham. Hopton's readiness to fight can be gauged by the readiness with which he moved on Farnham itself, as soon as he knew of Waller's whereabouts. Deploying his army before Farnham Castle, Hopton did his best to draw Waller into battle. Failing to do so, he withdrew 6 miles to Odiham.

Before settling into winter quarters himself, Hopton resolved to make use of Waller's absence by taking Arundel, and so establish a foothold in Sussex. Having succeeded, he resolved to secure Romsey as a base for a future assault on the Roundhead stronghold of Southampton, and may have done so, but for the fact that Waller had no intention of remaining immobile at Farnham while all this was going on. Hopton had decided to split his army for the duration of the winter, with forces at Winchester, Alresford, Alton and Petersfield. By making one of his famous night marches, Waller advanced from Farnham on the evening of 12 December to surprise the Alton garrison before dawn the following day. The operation was a great success, and after some particularly bitter fighting, the Roundheads took the town.

Now it was Waller's turn to make rapid progress. On 17 December he marched on Arundel. This time, there was no element of surprise, but after an artillery bombardment of the Royalist defences, the Roundhead infantry stormed the earthworks. Again, although the town was fiercely contested, the Royalists eventually gave way, retiring into the castle which was starved into surrender on 6 January. The year 1643 ended on a high note as far as military operations in the south were concerned. Even better news was to arrive from the north as the new year began.

The Road to Cheriton

In his *Battles in Britain 1642–1746* William Seymour draws attention to the problems inherent in any study of the Battle of Cheriton. The exact location of the fighting itself has, comparatively recently, become a matter of dispute, while the preliminary moves can be confusing owing to conflicting contemporary accounts. This may be a contributory reason for its omission from some of the standard battlefield texts. In order to grasp the essentials of the campaign, a measure of simplification is necessary.

In January 1644 the Scots entered the war on the side of Parliament, thus weakening the hand of the peace party. With 20,000 men under his command, Alexander Leslie had marched across the border. Snow lay thickly on the ground and Leslie's action was one of several throughout the war years which signified an end to the traditional seasonal inactivity when armies were supposed to be tied to winter quarters.

Keen to build on this advantage in every possible way, Parliament gave priority to furnishing Waller with an army with which he could take on Hopton. By mid-March 1644 their efforts had been so successful that Waller was able to launch his fresh campaign at the head of 3,000 horse, 600 dragoons and 5,000 infantry, with the promised additional support of 1,800 horse and dragoons under Sir William Balfour. On 27 March the new Roundhead army was mustered at East Meon, 4 miles to the west of Petersfield.

Hopton, meanwhile, had used the winter months to revitalize his army with new recruits, raising his strength to some 2,000 horse and 2,000 infantry. Reinforced at Winchester by the septuagenarian Earl of Forth, who assumed nominal command, the Royalist army now totalled 3,800 horse and 3,200 infantry. On 26 March this force left Winchester with the intention of surprising some Roundhead horse and infantry quartered at Warnford, a manoeuvre which, although unsuccessful, did have the effect of bringing Waller out into the open.

With his army deployed on high wooded ground immediately to the west of East Meon, Waller was hoping to entice Hopton up the hill in a repeat of the Lansdown action. Instead, with his own army formed up on Old Winchester Hill, Hopton dispatched some cavalry in an attempt to draw the Roundheads down but, apart from allowing some skirmishing, Waller refused to be drawn; he decided to make a dash for Alresford. The thinking behind this manoeuvre is not readily apparent. In the long term, the possession of Alresford, on the main London–Winchester road, would be advantageous but, in the present stand-off situation, there could be no immediate benefits. Perhaps Waller was seeking to gain some real or illusory tactical advantages.

On 21 March Prince Rupert had relieved Newark. Forced to send more troops northward, Parliament had instructed Waller not to engage in a major battle unless he possessed a clear advantage – so, in withdrawing, he may have been merely following instructions. Whatever the reason for his move, Hopton was having none of it, and set off in pursuit. There then developed another not unusual phenomenon: two opposing armies, less than 1 mile apart, marching almost in parallel towards their common objective, the Roundheads via the village of Bramdean, the Royalists via Hinton Ampner. The Royalist rate of progress was such that they overtook Waller's horse, and when they realized that the race was won, they halted at Tichborne, 2 miles to the south of Alresford. Waller halted at Hinton Ampner.

On the following day, 28 March, there was some skirmishing in the area as both sides reconnoitred the ground. Colonel Sir George Lisle was ordered to establish a forward post on high ground to the north of Waller's position. Waller himself remained inactive because his Council of War had difficulty in reaching a decision. Some, heeding Parliament's advice, urged caution – even retreat – though others, including Waller, mindful of his numerical advantage over the Royalist army, wanted to fight. In the end, it was decided to stand fast. As a first step towards deployment, a strong force of musketeers under Lieutenant-Colonel Walter Leighton was detailed to take Cheriton Wood.

The Battle of Cheriton

The morning of 29 March was misty, enabling Leighton's musketeers, in the opening move of the battle, to reach Cheriton Wood unobserved, a fact which Hopton realized when the sound of musket fire reached his ears. Lisle, his position threatened, was forced to withdraw.

The Earl of Forth marshalled his forces on the ridge to the south of Tichborne, and Hopton sent 1,000 musketeers under Colonel Appleyard to take the wood. Although supported by artillery, Appleyard could make little headway until one of his divisions, led by Lieutenant-Colonel Edward Hopton, outflanked the Roundheads. Caught in a cross-fire, they retreated,

The battlefield of Cheriton. The relatively recently sited battlefield monument is in the foreground. The gently undulating ground to the right of Cheriton Wood constituted the arena for the main action.

The armour and accoutrements of Sir Arthur Hesilrige's regiment of cuirassiers, or 'lobsters' as, for obvious reasons, they were popularly known. When Hesilrige was surrounded at Roundway Down, his assailants could make no impression upon him with either sword or pistol – an incident which caused King Charles to remark that had he been provisioned as well as he was fortified, he might have withstood a lengthy siege. (Mansell Collection)

leaving Appleyard in possession. Encouraged by this success, Hopton wanted to attack but Forth, worried about the Roundhead's numerical supremacy, thought it unwise. Thus, they remained strung out over the lower ridge with Forth's infantry on the right, Hopton's on the left and with cavalry on both flanks.

Waller's army, meanwhile, was now ranged across the ridge crossed by Lamborough Lane, the infantry in the middle with cavalry commanded by Hesilrige and Balfour, to left and right respectively, on the lower ground in front.

It is difficult to guess how the battle would have developed if commands had been obeyed. There might have been no battle at all. However, during the late morning, an impetuous Royalist commander, Sir Henry Bard, led his regiment forward, on his own authority, to attack Hesilrige's horse. As soon as Bard's men were well clear of their own lines, the 'lobsters' advanced and cut them off, killing or capturing them all.

Begun in confusion, the battle now developed in similar vein. More troops from the Royalist right wing descended into the valley, with men from the Roundhead left descending to meet them. Their movement restricted to the narrow bridleways, the Royalists were unable to deploy, and by early afternoon, it was clear that their position was untenable.

Waller's right wing had been unable to stray too far owing to the presence of Appleyard's musketeers in Cheriton Wood, until Colonel Walter Slingsby, commanding infantry to the left of the Royalist line, obligingly launched an assault on Balfour's position. In the mêlée which followed, the Royalist infantry stood firm, repulsing Balfour's counter-charge, but Appleyard, unable to distinguish between friend and foe, could offer little support. As Slingsby's infantry slowly began to give way, Hopton dispatched Sir Edward Stowell's brigade of 1,000 horse to render assistance but, again, the necessity of proceeding down the narrow Bramdean Lane ruled out effective deployment. The confusion grew, with Waller himself in the thick of the fighting, narrowly avoiding capture. Stowell's brigade was badly mauled, with Stowell himself, suffering from several wounds, being taken prisoner.

Hopton had accompanied Stowell into the valley – one wonders whether he and Waller caught sight of one another – and knew that the time to retreat was not far off. Somehow, Hopton managed a reasonably orderly withdrawal to the hill, where he found Forth already making arrangements for the army's departure. The only discernible panic was in the ranks of Appleyard's musketeers, who threw down their weapons and came streaming out of the wood. The fear that the Roundheads would engage in hot pursuit proved unfounded, the cautious Waller insisting on regrouping.

Forth remained with the Royalist infantry on Tichborne Down to cover the retreat of his guns and supply wagons. To confound any pursuit, it was decided to split the army under cover of darkness, with Hopton taking the infantry to Basing House while Forth and the cavalry set off at a brisk pace towards Winchester – a strategy which succeeded in confounding the 'Night Owl'.

The Aftermath

As usual, estimates of casualties varied enormously. Initial wildly exaggerated accounts speak of 10,000 Royalists killed and captured. A more reliable figure would be in the region of 300 dead. Although estimates of as few as thirty Roundheads killed would have to be scaled up, Royalist casualties were certainly much heavier. The Royalists lost more men 'of note' but, again, this often happened and may merely reflect the social composition of the Royalist army. Perhaps one should spare a thought for the wounded, condemned to endure the rigours of primitive field surgery: Captain Euble Floyd, 'wounded in ye very midst of his backe'; Captain Raoul Fleury, whose foot was shot off by a cannon ball; Colonel Thompson whose leg was amputated; Major Bovill, 'wounded in the belly that he cannot live'.

With casualties comparatively light, the Royalists did not place overdue emphasis on the result, and Parliament realized that although it relieved the pressure on London, their victory was in no way decisive. Looking back on the battle, some have argued that it represented a watershed in the conflict, with the Royalists being pushed back on to the defensive. At the time, this did not appear to be the case, the Earl of Essex dismissing Waller's triumph as an isolated victory of little consequence. To an extent, Essex's criticism of Waller was based upon resentment, but any fears he may have entertained that Waller's star was in the ascendant were soon to be quelled.

The day after the battle, Waller had entered Winchester, to be presented with the keys of the city by the mayor, watched by the Royalist garrison which had taken refuge in Winchester Castle. That night Waller marched as far as Stockbridge, 9 miles to the west. His masters wished him to proceed directly to the West Country, but this he failed to do, getting no further than Christchurch. The problems he faced were not new to him, part of his army – the London Brigade – having refused to do anything until they were paid. Delays in the dispatch of the required funds, requested by Waller immediately after Cheriton, led to the disgruntled Londoners returning home. Just as Langdale's Royalist Northern Horse disliked going south, the London Trained Bands had no stomach for fighting in the west. With the removal of the immediate threat to the capital, they saw little point in carrying on. Thus Waller retreated with them to Farnham and thence to London, where he planned to put his case for having his army suitably reinforced and equipped so as to allow him to undertake his mission.

The Royalists, meanwhile, were more immediately concerned with the possibility that Hopton's defeat had opened the door to an attack on their own capital of Oxford. At a council of war, Prince Rupert suggested a holding action around Oxford, while he himself went north to relieve pressure on the Duke of Newcastle, besieged in York. The Royalist garrison at Reading was evacuated, the 2,500 troops being used to bolster the Oxford garrison. By mid-May both Waller and Essex, commanding separate armies, were on the move. Although, as might be expected, cooperation between them was at a premium, they took Reading on 19 May.

Without waiting for the expected assault on Oxford, Charles led his army out of the city and marched through the Cotswolds to Worcester. As he had hoped, Waller and Essex, in pursuit, quarrelled and Essex marched off to the south west to attempt the relief of Lyme, besieged by Prince Maurice. This left Waller and the king to jockey for position, the armies eventually meeting on 29 June at Cropredy Bridge where the Royalists scored a distinct success and dealt a blow to Waller's reputation from which the victor of Cheriton never fully recovered. As his victory at Lansdown had led to defeat at Roundway Down, so Cheriton, it seemed, had paved the way for Cropredy Bridge.

The Walk

Distance: 4 miles (6.44 km)

Begin in Cheriton, a picturesque village straddling the B3046. The general stores (and post office) is situated on a side-road by the village green. Branching off this side-road, in turn, is a small access road – look for the Freeman's Yard sign – alongside which runs the River Itchen. At the end of this road is a gravel drive leading to Cheriton House, to the left of which is a well marked public footpath, the starting point for the walk (Pathfinder 1264 584285) (Point A).

Walk up this narrow path, bordered by high fences on either side. Shortly it opens out into the fields. On reaching the fence at the top, one is rewarded with a splendid view of the battlefield with high ground to both north and south, occupied by Royalists and Roundheads respectively, and Cheriton Wood directly ahead. Negotiate the stile and follow the path to the right

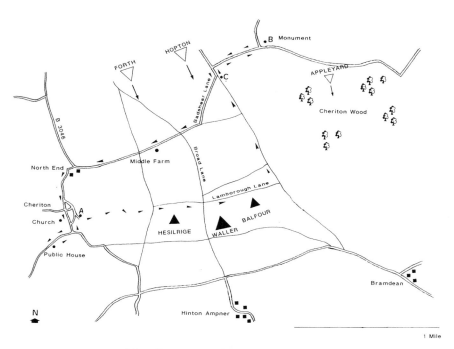

The Battle of Cheriton, 1644

around the field perimeter. Continue on, crossing Hinton Lane, with Middle Farm on the left. Hesilrige's cavalry would have descended across one's line of progress from the right. Continue over Broad Lane and, passing through the gate ahead, keep on towards Cheriton Wood. Waller would have occupied the ridge along this stretch of track and no more than a glance is required to appreciate that the descent to the centre of the battlefield is quite a steep one.

On reaching the trees – at the time of the battle, this portion of woodland was open ground – turn to the left so as to follow the track up towards the Royalist positions. For once, the Ordnance Survey map battlefield symbol accurately marks the centre of the action (Pathfinder 1264 599293). Continue past the private farm track on the left and on up to the staggered junction with Badshear Lane and Cheriton Lane. Bear right into Cheriton Lane and, a little way along, at the Bishops Sutton junction, view the battlefield memorial (Pathfinder 1243 600302) (Point B). This stretch of road affords another excellent view of the main arena, the land dipping to a gentle hollow between the two ridges – the favoured topography for Civil War cavalry engagements. Appleyard's musketeers would have advanced on Cheriton Wood from a point to the left of the memorial.

Return to Badshear Lane junction, crossing what would have been the path of Stowell's cavalry as it rode, regiment by regiment, towards the Roundhead guns. Carry on down Badshear Lane. The point at which the road crosses Broad Lane assists identification of the line of Bard's suicidal charge at Hesilrige's lines (Pathfinder 1264 592294) (Point C).

Carry on past Middle Farm and walk on to North End and the junction with the B3046. Turn right and continue to the Saxon church (Pathfinder 1264 582285) which has an interesting collection of brasses. Emerging from the church, walk up to the Beauworth junction and turn to the right. A little way along, on the left-hand side, is the Flowerpots public house, where refreshment may be taken. Return to the B3046 and turn right. Further along the road, to the left of the main entrance to Cheriton House, is a grass footpath, running alongside the River Itchen, which leads back to the starting point.

The area as a whole provides for excellent walking and, as will be noted, includes portions of the Wayfarer's Walk, a 70 mile long-distance path running from the Hampshire/Berkshire border down to the south coast. As the rights of way are accurately defined on Pathfinder 1264, it is possible for the enterprising rambler to expand or contract the suggested battlefield walk, as desired.

By way of conclusion, it may be added that the network of ancient tracks covering the battlefield is said to be haunted by the ghosts of fallen Royalists, while participants in Sealed Knot Society re-enactments of the battle have remarked upon the curious sensation of being assisted in their labours by unseen figures from the past.

Further Explorations

Hampshire is rich in Civil War associations. Ten miles to the north east of Cheriton, along the A31, is Alton (Landranger 186 7139), scene of a sharp encounter between Waller and Lord Crawford. In the evening of 12 December 1643 Waller launched a surprise attack on the Royalist-held town. Crawford, accompanied by his cavalry, made himself scarce, leaving his infantry to bear the brunt of the Roundhead assault. They stood little chance in Alton's narrow streets and the survivors, under the command of Colonel Richard Bolle, fell back on the Church of St Laurence where they made a last stand. From the churchyard they were pressed back into the church itself, where the battle continued until Bolle himself, directing operations from the pulpit, was overcome and beaten to death. The exterior of the church still bears the marks of Roundhead musket balls and Bolle's sacrifice is commemorated by a plaque. The Royalist dead were buried in the churchyard by the north wall, while several hundred survivors were taken prisoner.

Hampshire was also the scene of the most celebrated siege of the war: the Siege of Basing House (Landranger 185 6652) near Basingstoke. Basing had started life as a Norman castle, subsequent developments leading to the creation of what became known as the 'Old House'. During the sixteenth century, the 1st Marquess of Winchester developed the site still further by adding a fortified mansion, the 'New House'. Surrounded by a high wall and a moat, the estate withstood all assaults for three years, from 1642 to 1645. Held for the Royalists by the 5th Marquess of Winchester, Basing was first invested by Waller in November 1643. Defeated by heavy rain and poor troop morale, the Roundheads were forced to withdraw. Partly as a means of salvaging something from the failed expedition, Waller launched his attack on Alton. Throughout the latter half of 1644, Basing was continuously under siege until a mixture of bad weather and Royalist pressure forced another withdrawal. As it continued to absorb everything the enemy could throw at it, Basing acquired a symbolic importance far outweighing its strategic value until, at one stage, nearly 20,000 Roundhead troops were committed to its fall. Finally, in the autumn of 1645, with the king no longer able to spare men and resources, Cromwell arrived on the scene. Was there ever a man with a greater talent for arriving at the right place at the right time? After allowing his men to loot St Mary's Church in Basing (Landranger 185 6652) he began a six-day artillery bombardment which succeeded in breaching the walls, allowing Roundhead troops to pour in. Among the Royalists taken prisoner was the architect, Inigo Jones, who had been responsible for the design of many additional fortifications which had kept the besiegers at bay. The customary process of wanton destruction which followed the fall of Basing House reduced it to rubble. The site may still be viewed, along with Cromwell's ghost which has, from time to time, been seen wandering in the locality.

Odiham (Landranger 186 7451), 7 miles to the east of Basing House, was held for Parliament. Royalists, on an excursion from Basing House, launched what they thought would be a surprise raid on the garrison on 31 May 1644. In fact, the Roundheads were expecting them and the attacking force, badly mauled, was forced to retire. The dining room of the George Inn in Odiham's High Street contains a chimney-piece allegedly taken from the ruins of Basing House. As it was common practice for folk to salvage rubble and whatever building materials they could find in the ruins of a slighted mansion, there may be some truth in the story.

Further Information

Notwithstanding its quiet atmosphere, Cheriton is quite a substantial village, its length augmented by North End to the north and New Cheriton to the south. The B3046 on which it stands, although quite a busy road, is not easy to find. It can be approached from Junction 6 of the M3, but this involves a detour into Basingstoke via the A339. Alternatively, it may be approached via Junction 9 of the M3 (which dovetails with the A34 at this point) by taking the A31. As the A31 is a dual carriageway which does not permit right turns, one has to thread one's way through New Alresford, keeping a watchful eye for Cheriton signposts. Parking is available on the access road by Freeman's Yard, the starting point for the walk. Early arrivals may find space by the post office/general stores on the village green.

Alton has a railway station, with direct services of a little over one hour's duration from London (Waterloo). At Alton, one may board a steam train to Alresford. This service, affectionately known as 'The Watercress Line' is operated by the Mid-Hampshire Railway. The line between Alton and Winchester via Alresford was originally opened in 1865 and staved off closure until 1973. In 1977 the section between Alresford and Ropley was re-opened, to be followed by the additional stretch of track to Alton. For details of services, telephone 01962 733810.

A separate service operates between London (Waterloo) and Winchester. Telephone 0171 262 6767 for details of Alton–London (Waterloo) and Winchester–London (Waterloo). Inter-City Cross Country links Winchester with many other major cities. For further information, telephone 01707 332945.

For details of bus services to Cheriton from Alton and Winchester, telephone 01962 868944. National Express coach services operate between Alton and Winchester and London (Victoria), telephone 0990 808080.

Definitive reading is provided by John Adair's *Cheriton 1664: The Campaign and The Battle*. A more general account is included in Adair's *Roundhead General: A Military Biography of Sir William Waller*. Useful chapters devoted to the battle may also be found in Rogers' *Battles and Generals of the Civil Wars*, Seymour's *Battles in Britain 1642–1746* (illustrated with the customary invaluable aerial photography) and Burne's *More Battlefields of England*. Ordnance Survey maps of the area are Landranger 185 and Pathfinders 1264 and 1265 (both of which are required).

A Tourist Information Office is located in Guildhall, The Broadway, Winchester, telephone 01962 8740500.

10
THE BATTLE OF LANGPORT
10 July 1645

Introduction

The Battle of Naseby lasted only three hours, but the outcome confirmed what everyone knew: the English Civil War was drawing to a close, with Parliament the inevitable victor. The Royalists made a splendid stand against the cool, professional New Model Army, but enthusiasm proved to be no substitute for astute leadership. Charles had made two mistakes. The first was in permitting Prince Rupert to front the Royalist right wing instead of insisting on his presence at the helm. The second error lay in allowing Goring, with his 3,000 cavalry – which would have been invaluable at Naseby – to continue operations in the West Country.

The king's preoccupation with the West Country was understandable as throughout the war it formed his main power base, Devon and Cornwall, most of Somerset and almost all of Wales remaining Royalist to the bitter end. Moreover, Goring considered the west his own personal preserve, expressing only a limited interest in events further afield. In view of this, coupled with the continuous friction which occurred between Goring and Prince Rupert, the king's decision can at least be understood, if not endorsed. As it turned out, while the king's army had been defeated, Goring's army remained intact. Now all Royalist hopes were pinned on Goring's performance. Although he would enjoy his pivotal role, his fitness for it remained open to question.

Events in Northamptonshire had no immediate repercussions on the Royalist position in the south west. With the exception of Taunton, Somerset was firmly for the king and for twelve months the Royalists had been chiselling away at Taunton's defences, with the garrison living in a state of perpetual siege. Goring thought he could deliver the knock-out blow, and was happily directing operations at Taunton when the news of the Naseby disaster reached him. At about the same time, he also learned of the approach of Fairfax and the New Model Army which had been ordered to march to Taunton's relief.

Instead of engaging Fairfax, Goring was instructed to delay him until the king had undertaken a recruitment drive. In the long term, Charles hoped to import French and Irish troops, but such plans, if they came to fruition at all, would have no bearing on Goring's immediate needs. Allegedly making every effort to muster fresh recruits in Wales, Charles spent his days playing bowls in the security of Raglan Castle. Perhaps his thoughts were already turning to Scotland and the victories of the Marquess of Montrose. While the king considered the possibility of marching north to link up with Montrose, Prince Rupert, dispatched to Bristol, and Goring were left to do what they could to rescue the Royalist cause in the west. In desperation, Goring turned to the 'Clubmen'.

The outrages committed by both Roundheads and Cavaliers were widespread. It was not unusual for soldiers to help themselves, quite brazenly, to the livestock and personal property of defenceless civilians. Although offenders were sometimes punished, implementation of codes of discipline was often difficult, particularly when army supplies and pay were overdue. At length, the countryfolk of the western counties introduced their own neighbourhood watch schemes which, by the spring of 1645, had developed into a substantial, well organized force. As a rule, the 'Clubmen' – so-called because they went armed with staves – found themselves fighting Goring's undisciplined Royalists, yet Goring entertained hopes that some of them would join him. Fairfax had more success, treating the Clubmen firmly but fairly, and they realized that the Roundheads were their best hope as far as the restoration of peace and stability was concerned. Thus Goring's army remained under-strength, hovering about Langport, waiting for non-existent reinforcements. Little wonder, then, if the general sought solace in the bottle.

The Road to Langport

On 5 July 1645 Fairfax reached Crewkerne, having put to flight a Royalist cavalry patrol nearby. From prisoners taken at this skirmish, it was learned that Goring was in possession of the bridges over the River Yeo at Ilchester and the River Parrett at Langport, thus safeguarding his line of retreat to Bridgwater. Fairfax decided to concentrate his army at Crewkerne and ordered Massey and Weldon to join him. That same day, Goring was camped at Somerton having, in fact, established a whole series of defensive positions along the River Yeo – at Yeovil and Long Load – and the River

Parrett – at Burrow Bridge and Petherton Bridge – in addition to those at Ilchester and Langport.

Colonel Charles Fleetwood, sent by Fairfax on a reconnaissance mission to Petherton, chanced upon a party of Royalists on the north bank of the Parrett. On seeing Fleetwood, the Royalists hurriedly retreated, allowing him to cross. Scouting further afield, Fleetwood discovered strong Royalist defences at the Yeo's crossing points at Long Load and Ilchester.

The Roundheads spent 6 July, a Sunday, in rest and prayer. On Monday 7 July Fairfax held a Council of War. Just as Fairfax rarely missed Sunday worship, so he never embarked on a major military operation without holding a Council of War. These councils, encompassing the general staff and regimental commanders, consisted of full and open discussions in which decisions were arrived at in as democratic a manner as circumstances allowed. On this occasion, it was decided to march to Yeovil. On arrival, the Roundheads discovered that the bridge over the Yeo had been destroyed. Once again, however, the Royalists on the opposite bank withdrew, leaving the enemy to make preparations to cross on the following day.

In the event, no crossing was made, intelligence being received to the effect that the Ilchester garrison had set fire to the town before withdrawing. Therefore Fairfax ordered the New Model Army to march back to Ilchester and cross the Yeo there. No sooner had they taken possession of the town than Fairfax learned that Goring had divided his force. Using Langport as

Lieutenant-Colonel Edward Massey. Best known as Governor of Gloucester during the siege of the city, Massey also played an important part in events leading up to the Battle of Langport. His victory at Isle Abbots resulted in the capture of two hundred Royalists, including several officers. However, it also meant that he arrived at Langport when the battle was well under way. Parliament's ultimate victory in the Civil War owed much to commanders like Massey who achieved success in countless minor engagements, while not participating in the celebrated set-piece battles.

his base, the Royalist commander had dispatched three brigades of cavalry under Lieutenant-General George Porter towards Taunton. The reason for this action is unclear. Goring may have intended to catch the Roundhead garrison at Taunton unawares; he may have decided to use Porter's men as a flank guard; he may have hoped to use Porter as a decoy to draw off some of Fairfax's troops; he may have been indulging in one of his alleged bouts of drunkenness. Whatever the reason, Fairfax did send 4,500 cavalry under Major-General Sir Edward Massey, the hero of the Siege of Gloucester, in pursuit.

In the afternoon of 9 July, Massey caught up with Porter at Isle Abbots, about 6 miles to the east of Langport. Catching the Royalists off guard, Massey put them to flight, killing about fifty and taking many prisoners in the process. Goring rode out from Langport in time to stage a rearguard action to cover the retreat of the survivors from Porter's command. Goring himself was slightly wounded.

With Massey to his rear, Goring's concern was that continued inactivity would result in his being boxed in. Under the circumstances, he thought it best to send on his supplies to Bridgwater, while he remained at Langport, intending to follow the baggage train as soon as it was expedient to do so. Fully expecting to have to fight a defensive battle, he wanted to be able to choose his own ground. Fairfax had to decide whether to withdraw, his own supplies now running low, or to draw up his men in front of Langport to 'do further as opportunity might be'. A Council of War opted for the latter course of action.

The Battle of Langport

On the morning of 10 July 1645 Goring arrayed his men on Ham Down, in the region of Furpits Lane, infantry to the fore, cavalry to the rear. Some 2,000 musketeers were deployed along the hedges bordering the narrow Langport–Somerton road. In response, Fairfax drew up his troops on Pitney Hill. As with Goring's army, the cavalry was flanked by infantry and musketeers. Fairfax had numerical superiority, with around 10,000 men opposing Goring's 8,000. Goring, it should be remembered, had envisaged a holding action to cover the withdrawal of his artillery and supplies to Bridgwater. Thus he retained only two guns.

At about 11.00 a.m., Fairfax decided to attack. In retrospect, this seems foolhardy. The ground on either side of the road being marshy and unsuitable for cavalry, the only way forward was along the well defended road. However, the Roundhead artillery soon silenced the Royalist guns,

Looking towards Pitney Hill, where Fairfax drew up his troops. The road – the present-day B3153 – up which the Roundhead cavalry charged was much narrower than it is today, with Royalist musketeers lining the hedges.

and Goring must have wished he had sent them on to Bridgwater. To clear a path for his cavalry, Fairfax sent forward 1,500 musketeers on either side of the road to deal with the Royalist musketeers. According to some accounts, the latter put up a fierce resistance, only gradually being forced to give ground. In contrast, Sir Richard Bulstrode maintained that many of the defenders simply ran away.

When the hedges had been all but cleared, 400 Roundhead horse under the command of Major Christopher Bethel charged forward on their unenviable errand. First they had to descend Pitney Hill, then clear the ford at the bottom before proceeding uphill along the lane, which was wide enough to take a maximum of only four horsemen riding abreast, with the objective of taking on a strong cavalry force waiting for them on Ham Down.

Remarkably, Bethel made it, his men emerging from the lane to right and left. The will to fight seems to have deserted the Royalist cavalry, for Bethel forced them to give ground. A counter-charge momentarily redressed the balance, but the lane was now open to allow Roundhead reinforcements through. Support in the shape of three troops of horse commanded by Major John Desborough appeared on the scene to consolidate Bethel's bridge-head. When Fairfax threw in his infantry and musketeers, the Royalists took to their heels, some retreating through Langport while others made directly for Bridgwater.

Hoping to delay their pursuers, those who retreated via Langport set fire to the town, but Cromwell, always in at the kill, still managed to catch up to take prisoners and supplies. The retreat to Bridgwater was more successful, with the Royalist cavalry fighting an almost continuous rearguard action.

Casualties were light, with about 300 Royalist dead against only about thirty Roundheads. Naturally, Bethel's troop of horse sustained the highest number of casualties on the Roundhead side, Bethel himself losing part of a hand. Among the 2,000 Royalist prisoners were many men of rank, including Sir Arthur Slingsby. As Rogers puts it in *Battles and Generals of the Civil War*, the Royal Army of the West, for practical purposes, had ceased to exist.

The importance of the Roundhead guns in the engagement should not be underestimated. Once the Royalist guns were silenced, Fairfax's artillery was able to concentrate on Goring's cavalry. Compelled to draw back from the brow of the hill, they were unable to offer their musketeers any support. In addition, Bethel's men were given a little more time and space to deploy when they emerged from the lane. But nothing should detract from what was a bold decision by Fairfax. What was fêted as a famous victory could so easily have ended in a disaster of the proportions suffered by the Royalists in the narrow lanes of East Down at Cheriton a year before.

The Aftermath

The Battle of Langport was the last large-scale battle of the First Civil War. Broken and dispirited, Goring's men no longer represented a threat to the all-conquering New Model Army. Fairfax quickly followed up his victory with a devastating assault on Bridgwater, after which the Royalist garrison at Bath was quick to surrender. In fact, Bridgwater had been pounded into a mass of rubble, its citizens pleading with the Royalist governor, Sir Hugh Wyndham, to surrender in order to save the town from total annihilation. Wyndham, with no expectation of additional support, agreed. Goring, who could have reinforced the garrison, had seemed confident of its ability to hold out, and had withdrawn to Barnstaple. His attachment to the bottle had long been remarked upon and it seems that this final error of judgement launched him on a 'bender', the effects of which caused the morale of his troops to hit an all-time low.

In company with the other Royalist commanders, Goring knew that the end was near. Even Prince Rupert now wished to sue for peace, yet the king remained obdurate. With Montrose scoring a string of successes in Scotland

and with the port of Bristol still in Royalist hands, Charles felt that victory was perhaps yet not beyond reach. Unfortunately, these glimmers of hope were doomed to be extinguished. Spectacular though they might be, the ephemeral victories of Montrose did not result in territorial gains, and the king's march northward to join him faltered at Doncaster. However, the final, crushing blow came with the fall of Bristol.

Rupert had confidently assured his uncle of his ability to hold Bristol, which he had captured two years earlier, for at least four months – an overconfident assertion for, as the king later pointed out, he failed to hold out for even four weeks. On 21 August Fairfax and Cromwell, at the head of an army 12,000 strong, arrived to lay siege to the city. A naval blockade of the mouth of the Severn ensured that the Royalist garrison was cut off by both land and sea. In the early hours of 10 September, negotiations for an honourable surrender having come to naught, Fairfax stormed the defences. With only 1,500 men at his disposal, Rupert found his lines severely overstretched and, following a heavy artillery bombardment, the Roundheads broke through into the town at a point where the defensive wall was only 5 ft in height. All who refused to surrender were put to the sword and Rupert realized that the futility of continued resistance could lead only to a great slaughter. Accordingly, he capitulated. The generous terms of the surrender allowed for the garrison's departure, complete with their horses and swords, and in the case of Rupert's lifeguards, their firearms. Once again, the prince had managed to extricate his valuable veterans from a hopeless situation.

This point of view was not shared by Charles, whose response to the news verged on the hysterical. Anyone save Rupert would have been tried for treason, but the king contented himself with condemning his faithful nephew to exile. Lord Digby capitalized upon the situation by suggesting that Rupert had surrendered purely as means of fulfilling his desire to bring the conflict to a speedy conclusion. Digby even manufactured evidence intended to show that the prince had designs on the Crown, and it is a measure of Charles's naïvety that he believed it. The legendary series of stormy meetings between uncle and nephew which took place at Newark led, ultimately, to reconciliation and to genuine feelings of remorse on the prince's part.

The Walk

Distance: 3½ miles (5.63 km)

Langport has only one well established main street, starting (from the direction of neighbouring Huish Episcopi) with Hill Street, which develops

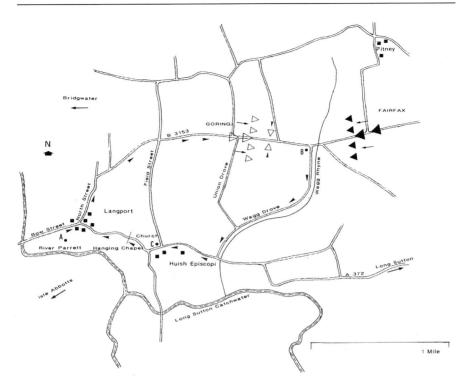

The Battle of Langport, 1645

into Cheapside which, in turn, becomes Bow Street. Begin at either of the two well marked public car parks, giving pedestrian access to the River Parrett (Pathfinder 1259 418268) (Point A). Walk eastwards, in the direction of the church, but branch off to the left, up North Street. Walk under the railway bridge and follow the road round to the right. The Royalist garrison was probably encamped in the triangular area defined today by North Street, the railway line and Field Street. Continue over the crossroads (the minor road to Wearne to the left, Field Street to the right) and walk up towards the Royalist positions. A little care is needed in places, but by keeping first to the left of the road and then crossing over to the right, progress can be made in relative safety. It was at the highest point along this road, the B3153, by the junction with the Low Ham road (Pathfinder 1259 433277) that Goring deployed his cavalry with artillery support.

Walk downhill towards Wagg Bridge. Ignore Union Drove on the right, surely one of the most alluring tracks ever to confront the determined rambler, and try to visualize the B3153 in terms of a narrow thoroughfare, lined with high hedges, behind which the Royalist musketeers waited patiently. The position occupied by Fairfax, on the slopes of Pitney Hill, appears to have been just as strong. The Roundhead cavalry, flanked by artillery, straddled the road to the rear of the musketeers. With the opposing forces occupying rising land divided by a depression, the setting, if not the battle itself, was not dissimilar in some respects to the battlefield at Naseby.

At Wagg Bridge (Pathfinder 1259 441275) (Point B) turn right and walk down the single-track Wagg Drove, bordering Wagg Rhine towards a suggested alternative site for the battle: Pathfinder 1259 gives a position based on the case for a long-vanished 'pass' at 438268, to the south of the railway bridge. The present-day landscape, much changed since the seventeenth century, does not help the investigator in attempts to establish the existence in this area of a lane crossing the Wagg Rhine. Certainly, no evidence presents itself to the naked eye.

Continue to the end of Wagg Drove and turn right towards Huish Episcopi. At the southern end of Field Street lies Huish Episcopi church (Pathfinder 1259 427267) (Point C) which, sadly, as a result of vandalism and theft, has had to close its doors to the casual visitor. One can, at least, admire the fifteenth-century tower – one of the finest in the country.

Instead of walking up Field Street, which takes through traffic away from Langport, continue on past the church, to enter the village via the Hanging Chapel, built for a medieval tradesmen's guild. A little way further along, the church (which will, again, very probably be locked), with its famous collection of medieval glass, seems to have been all but smothered by the buildings around it.

Walk down The Hill and on into the town, to enjoy refreshment at the Langport Arms. Once known as The Swan, it probably began life as a well-to-do merchant's house, the lounge boasting a fifteenth-century timber ceiling. With Langport conveniently situated on the London–Devonshire road, it also saw service as a coaching inn. Visiting Puritan ministers who came to preach in the town were entertained quite lavishly here. Emerging from the inn, turn left and walk back to the starting point.

Further Explorations

Mid-way between Langport and Bridgwater, on the A361, is Burrow Mump (Landranger 182 3530), the site of an early fortification, possibly one of King Alfred's forts. The fifteenth-century church on top of the hill is now a memorial to the men of Somerset who gave their lives in the First World

War. Used during the Civil War as a look-out post for troops guarding Burrow Bridge, fleeing Royalists sought refuge here after the Battle of Langport. The alleged connection with King Alfred is given some credence through the great Saxon warrior's association with nearby Athelney. According to the legends, it was here that he both burned the bread and disguised himself as a minstrel, so that he might spy upon the Danes (see p. 7). A monument marks the spot where he built an abbey to commemorate the ultimate success of his AD 877–8 campaign.

Immediately to the north of Langport are High Ham and Low Ham. The latter has a seventeenth-century church (Pathfinder 1259 433291) notable for its open aspect. In place of a churchyard is a conglomeration of embankments, the only remaining clue to a mansion which got little further than the drawing board. This portion of Somerset is also rich in Roman remains, a mosaic pavement having been excavated on nearby Hext Hill (Pathfinder 1259 435288).

Just over 1 mile to the south of Langport is the hamlet of Muchelney, and the remains of an eighth-century Benedictine abbey (Pathfinder 1259 428248). The cloisters and the abbot's lodging survived the Dissolution, the latter by being pressed into use as a farmhouse. A rare example of a fourteenth-century priest's house (Pathfinder 1259 431249) may also be viewed.

Seven miles to the east is the Roman town of Ilchester (Landranger 183 5123). Instead of the bustling market town into which many significant Roman settlements developed, one meets here a tranquil atmosphere of decaying gentility. Situated at the confluence of no less than five Roman roads, Ilchester did retain a measure of importance into the Middle Ages and was the birthplace of the thirteenth-century friar, philosopher and scientist, Roger Bacon. At nearby Yeovilton (Landranger 183 5423) is situated the Fleet Air Arm Museum, which records the history of the Royal Naval Air Service.

Swinging westward from Ilchester along the A303, a journey of 13 miles brings one to Ilminster (Landranger 193 3614). As its name implies, the town developed around the eighth-century minster situated on the River Isle and later recorded in the Domesday survey as belonging to Muchelney Abbey. The Reformation led to the lands being given to the Duke of Somerset. The present-day Church of St Mary contains the remains of Nicholas and Dorothy Wadham, founders of Oxford's non-conformist Wadham College. In the churchyard is a headstone commemorating two soldiers, Emanuel and Thara Hutchings. Emanuel was killed in 1855 in the Crimea, Thara in India during the Mutiny of 1857.

Non-conformity is deep-rooted in Ilminster. While Ilchester contributed only eight men to Monmouth's rebellion in 1685, fifty-four Ilminster men enlisted in the duke's ranks. Another well known Ilminster family, the Spekes, was openly supportive of Monmouth's cause, and Charles Speke was hanged after having been seen to shake hands with the duke in Ilminster's town square. In areas where non-conformity took hold, priests' holes can usually be found. In Ilminster two such hiding places have been uncovered in The Chantry.

Further Information

Langport is 10½ miles south east of Bridgwater on the A372. Motorists approaching from the east should leave the A372 at Huish Episcopi, to take the 'access only' road by the church in order to enter Langport via the Hanging Chapel. As noted in the Walk, there are two well marked public car parks on the left-hand side of the road beyond the Langport Arms. The farther one is usually less busy, and offers access to a riverside walk at the rear.

Langport was once served by two railway lines. The first, the Bristol & Exeter's Yeovil branch line, opened in 1853, has long since been dismantled. The station stood at the western extremity of the village, just across the River Parrett. The second, existing, line was a late starter in the railway stakes, not opening until 1906. However, as a more direct route to the south west (until then, it was necessary to travel via Bristol), it proved a success, with Langport East station situated at the north end of the town, near the North Street bridge. Today, Bridgwater and Yeovil are the most convenient rail heads. For details of services between London (Paddington) and Bridgwater, and between London (Waterloo) and Yeovil, telephone 0171 928 8080. For details of bus services from either destination to Langport, telephone 01823 255696. Bridgwater is also the destination of a number of National Express coach routes; for details of services, telephone 0990 808080.

Further reading is provided by Rogers in *Battles and Generals of the Civil Wars* and by Burne in *More Battlefields of England*. The latter volume includes a discussion of the issue of the alternative site for the engagement, as does a locally published booklet, *The Battle of Langport: A Short Historical Account* by Graham Edwards, which also merits perusal. Ordnance Survey maps of the area are Landranger 193 and Pathfinder 1259.

A Tourist Information Office can be found at the Podimore Service Area, at the junction of the A372 with the A303 (Landranger 183 5325). A local information centre (closed on Sundays) is attached to the second-hand bookshop in Langport.

11
THE BATTLE OF SEDGEMOOR
6 July 1685

Introduction

Sedgemoor has been described as the last battle to take place on English soil. Such a claim, however, discounts the battle which took place at Preston in 1715, the year of the first Jacobite rising. It has also been said that the battle which decided the fate of the Monmouth rebellion is more easily identifiable with battles of the English Civil War than with the great battles of the Hanoverian age: Sheriffmuir, Prestonpans and Culloden. In part, this is true, but the story of Sedgemoor does contain hints of things to come: famous regiments, such as the Grenadier Guards, the Coldstream Guards and the Royal Scots appear there, albeit in embryonic form; the famous red coat of the British Army appears on the field of battle, while body armour has all but disappeared; to a great extent, the musket is the weapon which determines the outcome of the battle, and the name Churchill rises to prominence.

The Monmouth rebellion grew out of the rivalry between Protestant and Catholic. The former was represented by the Whig party (named after the 'Whiggamores', Scotland's Presbyterian rebels), and the latter by the Tories (named after Irish Catholic rebels). The question of the succession dominated English politics for many years before the death of Charles II in 1685. Despite his sexual proclivity, it did not appear that the king intended fathering a legitimate heir to the throne. This meant that Charles's brother, James, Duke of York, a man with undoubted Papist sympathies, would succeed. In 1679 the leading Whig, the Earl of Shaftesbury, put forward a rather weak case for an alternative candidate: the king's eldest illegitimate son, James Scott, Duke of Monmouth. Charles was able to hold out against Shaftesbury because, unlike his father, he did not depend upon Parliament for money. Louis XIV, anxious to support the English monarch in his defence of the principle of hereditary right, kept him well supplied with funds.

Defeated politically, the leading Whigs resorted to subterfuge. In what became known as the Rye House Plot, they planned to murder Charles at Rye House, near Hoddesdon, as he returned from Newmarket races in April 1683. The plot failed and Monmouth, who had been involved, was exiled. For the next two years, the duke lived comfortably in Holland in the company of several other expatriots who had fallen foul of the government. Among this number was the Earl of Argyll, sentenced to death for his opposition to the Test Act of 1681, designed to exclude Presbyterians from public office.

When James became king following the sudden death of Charles in February 1685, Monmouth and Argyll set in motion a plot to exploit Protestant disaffection. While Argyll invaded Scotland, Monmouth would land in the south west of England, where, having toured successfully some years earlier, he planned to acquire the support of the local gentry. In addition, having seen extensive military service with the 1st Troop of Horse Guards, he hoped that he could count on the loyalty of men he had once commanded.

Argyll, at the head of a relatively strong force, landed on Kintire in May, and soon ran into trouble. Only a fraction of his promised support materialized and instead of heading south for the borders, he embarked on a disastrous march to Glasgow. Monmouth, in ignorance of the progress of his ally, was running well behind schedule, thus giving James a month's grace to raise an army. His main difficulty was the lack of sufficient funds. The handful of supporters who accompanied him on the venture were, like himself, all exiles, and destitute into the bargain. They included among their number Lord Grey and a lawyer, Nathaniel Wade, both implicated in the Rye House Plot, and several veterans of many anti-establishment plots including Robert Ferguson and Abraham Holmes. Only by beggaring himself and his mistress, Lady Henrietta Wentworth, who had accompanied him into exile, could Monmouth afford to cobble together the weakest of expeditionary forces. Such was the efficiency of King James's intelligence that by the time Monmouth's force sailed on 1 June 1685, the king's spies were well aware of both its strength and its destination.

The Road to Sedgemoor

Monmouth's road to Sedgemoor began at Lyme Regis where, to the delight of the general populace, he landed on 11 June 1685. For three days he remained there, gathering support. An initial sortie aimed at disposing of Royalist militia at Bridport met with mixed success and, in some respects, set the tone for the rest of the campaign – Lord Grey retreated in disarray while Nathaniel Wade, lacking cavalry support, offered stout resistance followed by an orderly withdrawal.

At last, on 15 June, the rebels moved out, marching to Axminster which they took with ease, the local militia fleeing at their approach. King James had expected the West Country militia to experience no difficulty in containing the insurrection but this, as his man on the spot, Colonel John Churchill, pointed out, represented a somewhat over-optimistic appraisal of the ability of these poorly organized amateurs. At Chard more than 150 men flocked to Monmouth's banner. At Taunton, perhaps the high point of his whole expedition, over 250 were added to the rebel ranks and Monmouth, burning his bridges, had himself proclaimed the rightful King of England. There could be no turning back.

An immediate assault on London being considered too risky, it was decided to march on Bristol. In so doing, the rebels would be taking the country's second largest city and also strengthening their West Country power base. Proceeding via Bridgwater, Glastonbury and Shepton Mallet, a route which encompassed Westonzoyland, the rebel army reached Pensford, 5 miles south of Bristol on 24 June. By this time, the column was being harried by regular cavalry under Churchill. Having despaired of the militia, James was now depending upon the regulars, with the Earl of Feversham, a cautious commander, having been appointed commander-in-chief. At first Feversham refused to believe that Monmouth intended attacking Bristol, and it was not until he had received first-hand evidence from another of his competent subordinates, Colonel Theophilus Oglethorpe, that he hurried from his lodging at Bath to superintend the great seaport's defences.

In the event, the rebel assault foundered at Keynsham, heavy rain making it impossible for them to use their muskets. The delay gave Monmouth pause for thought. In truth, he was worried about facing regular troops, having always trusted – erroneously – that the men he had once commanded would refuse to fight him. In addition, his support stemmed almost entirely from the agricultural and artisan classes. Without the backing of the landed gentry, the rebellion had little hope of ultimate success. In a move which smacked of defeat, the rebels turned away from Bristol, with a view to marching into Wiltshire, where it was hoped to pick up more recruits.

A general engagement very nearly took place at the village of Norton St Philip, between Bath and Frome, where the rebels camped on the night of 26 June. In the early hours of the following day, the Duke of Grafton, commanding 500 Royalist dragoons, attempted an audacious assault on the rebel camp. Caught unawares by the rebel defences, Grafton's men were trapped in a narrow lane and suffered heavy casualties. Both sides being reluctant to risk all, the situation failed to develop and the Royalists withdrew to Bradford-on-Avon. At length, Monmouth resumed his wanderings and took the rebels to Frome, where it was learned that Argyll's invasion had failed miserably, and Shepton Mallet, where it became apparent that enthusiasm for the cause was starting to wane, recruitment falling well below expectations. Finally, on 3 July, they found themselves back in Bridgwater, the militia having fled at their approach.

Deciding that the militia was more of a hindrance than a help, Feversham lightened his army by sending most of them away, and by 5 July was camped just 3 miles from Bridgwater, at Westonzoyland. It seemed that Monmouth was preparing for a siege but, cautious as ever, Feversham decided to wait and see. In fact, Monmouth had no intention of digging in, and until he learned of Feversham's proximity had planned to march north to Cheshire if he could throw Feversham off the scent.

Although Monmouth's force may have outnumbered the fitter and leaner Royalist army, it is probable that they were more evenly matched than is usually claimed, with Feversham now leading around 2,700 men and Monmouth in excess of 3,000. The Royalists were divided into what were to develop into several famous regiments: Dumbarton's (Royal Scots), 1st and 2nd Battalions of King's Guards (Grenadier Guards), 2nd Regiment of Guards (Coldstream Guards) and Queen Dowager's Regiment (West Surreys). The Royalist cavalry comprised Life Guards and Horse Grenadiers, in addition to the King's Regiment of Horse (Royal Horse Guards) and Churchill's Dragoons (Royal Dragoons). The rebel army, on the other hand, comprised Grey's cavalry and five infantry battalions commanded by Edward Matthews, Richard Buffet, Abraham Holmes, John Foulkes and the doughty Nathaniel Wade. Certainly arms were in short supply and many potential rebel recruits may well have been turned away for this very reason. Those rebels in possession of muskets had been inadequately trained, while a shortage of pikes led to the improvisation of scythe blades tied to rough-hewn staves, giving rise to a common misconception of the rebel rank and file as a motley assortment of village idiots with little to commend them save a tragically gauche commitment to a lost cause.

The Battle of Sedgemoor

The Royal army was first espied by Monmouth from the tower of St Mary's Church in Bridgwater. Camped hard by Westonzoyland, to the rear of the Bussex Rhine, one of the dykes which drained the moor, Feversham's position was well chosen. He himself, together with his cavalry, had set up his headquarters in the village, with the infantry occupying the forward

The battlefield monument at Sedgemoor, on a site which would have been occupied by
Feversham's infantry, to the east of the Bussex Rhine. St Mary's Church, Chedzoy, is to the left
of the monument, just below the skyline.

positions behind the dyke. Another portion of his force, the Wiltshire
militia, under the Earl of Pembroke, was based almost 2 miles away at
Middlezoy, while a forward post, commanded by Sir Francis Compton, was
established at Chedzoy.

Much has been made of Monmouth's decision to risk all by launching a
surprise night assault, historians being sharply divided on the wisdom of
such a course of action. Barrett is of the opinion that it was wise to attack
the enemy's infantry, isolated as it was from the cavalry, and Robin Clifton
thinks Monmouth's plan 'well considered', but Howard Green dismisses it
as a 'mad venture', with Young and Adair viewing it as 'truly astonishing'.
As the latter authors also point out, however, successful rebellions do not
comprise defensive actions. With Feversham's army out of the way, the road
to London would be open. Only by riding the crest of the wave of rebel
enthusiasm, always a short-lived phenomenon, could Monmouth hope to
succeed – hence his desperate gamble. In fact, the actual scheme seemed
sound enough. The rebel force outnumbered Feversham's army, which
slumbered unaware of the enemy's proximity. Only two factors militated
against the plan: the rebels were insufficiently disciplined for an orderly,
silent night march, and the local guide used by Monmouth proved
unreliable.

The plan began to founder almost before it was put into action, when it
was decided not to follow the direct route to Westonzoyland. Roughly
corresponding with the present-day A372, this was the road Monmouth had
traversed twice within the previous fortnight. Perhaps he thought that it

would be too well guarded and too obvious an approach. Instead, sometime after 10.00 p.m. on the evening of 5 July 1685, the rebel army moved out of Bridgwater in a north-easterly direction, along the present-day A39, with the aim of swinging around in a wide arc so as to descend on Westonzoyland from the direction from which they would be least expected.

To avoid Compton's outpost at Chedzoy it was necessary to sweep even further north before turning southward by Peasy Farm. Somehow, the ragtag army missed a Royalist scouting party, sent out for the very purpose of watching the Bristol road. With the help of their guide, a man by the name of Godfrey, the rebels managed to negotiate a drainage ditch known as the Black Dyke, but ran into trouble at the next ditch, the Langmoor Rhine, when Godfrey was unable to locate the point at which it could be crossed.

At this juncture, a pistol shot was heard. There are several explanations for the incident. A pistol may have been discharged accidentally by one of the rebels in the confusion; a Royalist harboured in the rebel ranks could have been trying to warn Feversham, or one of Compton's pickets may have caught sight of the straggling column. Whatever the cause, Compton was alerted and a messenger rode off to warn the main camp.

It now became important for Monmouth to make all haste and hit Feversham before the Royalist troops were able to gather their wits about them. Grey was dispatched with his horsemen to cross the Bussex Rhine, with Wade, heading the leading infantry battalion, being ordered to follow at his best speed. But fortune was not with Monmouth in the early hours of 6 July; in the darkness, Grey floundered in his attempts to find a place to cross the ditch. Faced with volleys of musket fire coming from the other side, the Royalists having succeeded in forming themselves into some kind of order, he had to retire. One contingent of rebel horse did manage to locate one of the two crossing points but, lacking the support of the main body of horse, they could make little impression on Compton's cavalry which had fallen back from Chedzoy and were now engaged in a spirited – and vital – defence of the crossing.

Wade, meanwhile, had also paused to muster his infantry into some sort of battle order. He had stopped well short of the Royalist lines, and the other battalions arriving alongside him found themselves drawn up to the right of the Westonzoyland camp. A concerted infantry assault might still have carried the day, but the rebels, assisted by three small field pieces, appeared to be content to stand their ground and return the Royalists' fire.

Slowly and deliberately, in a move in which Churchill seems to have played a role, the Royalists were deployed in the manner best suited to destroy the rebels as soon as dawn broke. Their own disciplined lines were shifted to the right, so as to face the rebels, and their own heavy artillery was brought into play. Well directed fire-power from both muskets and guns cut gaps in the rebel lines until, with the onset of daylight, Feversham could, at last, see that it was safe for him to go on to the offensive.

Colonel Oglethorpe's cavalry crossed the ditch to the right of the rebel lines, while the King's Royal Horse used the crossing by the Bridgwater road on the left. This pincer movement, supported by a frontal infantry assault over the ditch, created panic, and whatever semblance of order there had been dissolved as the rebel units disintegrated into a single fleeing mass. Many had never even reached the field of battle, having lingered in the rear when the fighting began. The remnant which fought on looked to their baggage train for ammunition, but the teamsters had fled. And in vain did they appeal to their leader, for he, too, had gone.

Most of the rebel casualties appear to have been sustained in the pursuit. The Royalist cavalry, fresh and eager, slaughtered several hundreds of the exhausted rabble as the latter scrambled desperately over fields and waded through ditches which impeded their progress while affording precious little cover. Many of those who lived through the day were herded into Westonzoyland church. Among the rebel commanders, only Wade kept his wits about him, managing to extricate 150 men and lead them to Bridgwater, where they dispersed.

Colonel Oglethorpe was given the honour of carrying tidings of the Royal success to London, while the victors amused themselves by indulging in an orgy of pre-trial hangings. In fact Feversham's success was short-lived and he drifted into obscurity, outshone by his brilliant subordinate, John Churchill, whose rise to fame was to usher in a new and terrible age in the development of warfare.

The Aftermath

Perhaps a thousand rebels died on the battlefield – and it would have been better for their leader had he been among them. In company with Grey, Monmouth made his way towards the south coast, hoping to buy a passage to the continent, but he was caught hiding in a ditch. Starving and exhausted, he had eluded capture for three days. Grey later saved his own life by informing on Monmouth who, in turn, hoped to cheat the executioner by informing on others. On 15 July 1685, however, his pleas for mercy having been dismissed, the duke was beheaded in an execution noted for its inefficiency, five or six blows of the axe being required to complete the job. Even then, according to Macauley, it was necessary to use a knife to completely separate the head from the shoulders.

The surviving rebel rank and file were even less fortunate for, as

A set of playing cards depicting events in the Monmouth rebellion was issued in 1685. The illustration accompanying the three of Clubs shows three rebels, one of whom is identified as 'Major Holmes' (Colonel Abraham Holmes) hanging in chains after summary execution. (British Museum)

common men, many were destined to meet traditional traitors' deaths by being hanged, drawn and quartered. Around 1,300 were taken prisoner on or near the battlefield. Confined in small West Country gaols, many with wounds left unattended, the vanquished waited throughout July and August. The places of those who died from their wounds or from disease were taken by new victims, whose suspected complicity in the rising was confirmed in the minds of their accusers by the tempting rewards on offer.

The man entrusted with meting out punishment was Lord Chief Justice Jeffreys, whose reputation as a hanging judge would be consolidated by his handling of the forthcoming series of trials. With an eye on promotion to the office of Lord Chancellor, Jeffreys proved anxious to oblige the king by delivering to the transgressors a short, sharp lesson is obedience to authority. This he achieved by less than creditable means, resorting to subterfuge in order to avoid the necessity of presiding over a thousand or so trials which could well drag on for a period of years. It was suggested to the prisoners that anyone who pleaded guilty as charged would be dealt with leniently, while 'obstinate' offenders would be punished accordingly – a policy which was amply demonstrated in Dorchester on 5 September, when thirteen out of thirty-five rebels who persisted in entering pleas of innocence were hanged two days afterwards, their tarred heads placed atop poles. The strategy worked: at

Taunton, for example, of 385 rebels tried on 18 September, only four pleaded not guilty.

Although some rebels were found not guilty, there seems to have been little rhyme or reason behind many of the verdicts. A few defendants at all the venues of the 'Bloody Assizes' – Dorchester, Exeter, Taunton and Wells – were freed, but it depended upon the luck of the draw rather than on the relative strengths and weaknesses of one's case. Similarly, of the hundreds who had thrown themselves on the king's mercy by admitting their presumed guilt, a proportion might have hoped to have their sentence of death commuted to transportation. In the final analysis, some 350 rebels were executed and around 850 sentenced to ten years' transportation to the West Indies.

Immediately after the rebellion, James launched plans for the creation of a standing army. Unfortunately for his own future, he ran this campaign in tandem with his attempts to promote Catholicism, and there were those who suspected, rightly or wrongly, that the two policies were not unconnected. Three years after Sedgemoor, the king was deposed in the bloodless 'Glorious Revolution' and was permitted to escape to France. Lord Chancellor Jeffreys, who also hoped to effect an escape, was captured, disguised as a seaman, at Wapping Old Stairs. He died a prisoner in the Tower of London while awaiting trial.

The Walk

Distance: 8 miles (12.88 km)

One main street, the A372, runs through the middle of Westonzoyland. Between the general stores and the Willow Tree Inn – closed at time of writing (1995) – cars may be parked at the roadside, so this makes a good starting point for the motorist (Pathfinder 1237 346349) (Point A). Take the A372 in the direction of Bridgwater. Walk out of the village past the cemetery, and take the rough track on the right. Along this track, about midway between the main road and the sewage works, stood the lower crossing point of the long-since vanished Bussex Rhine, used by Feversham's cavalry. Pathfinder 1237 347352 provides an approximate reference. Continue along the track, noticing on the left the solitary prefabricated building which provides one with a clue that a Second World War airfield was based at Westonzoyland (see p. 135). The Royalist army was deployed to the right, behind the Bussex Rhine.

A little way further on, the track veers sharply to the right. However, take

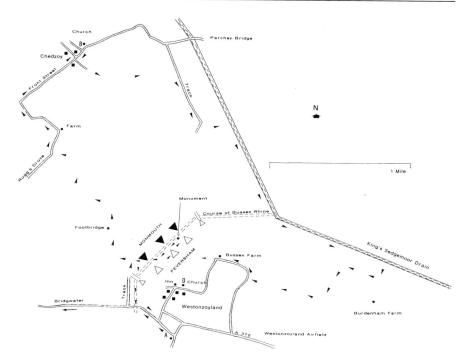

The Battle of Sedgemoor, 1685

the public footpath to the left. This involves climbing an old gate. Walk straight ahead along the hedgerow and on into the next field. Turn sharp right and follow the hedgerow up to Chedzoy New Cut. A new footbridge to the left (replacing the old bridge to the right, depicted on the Ordnance Survey map) takes one across the water. Continue straight on up to Moor Drove Rhine. The footpath system in the area has fallen into serious disrepair, with crops sown almost up to the hedgerow, with only a few signs that solitary ramblers labour to keep it open by irregular forays into the undergrowth.

On reaching Moor Drove Rhine, climb a second gate and turn to the left. A third gate, which also has to be climbed, at the end of this stretch bears a weather-beaten sign (on the other side) suggesting that this was once a well marked footpath. Follow the track (walking is now much easier) to emerge on to Rugg's Drove; follow it round into Front Street and on into Chedzoy.

At the top end of the village is St Mary's Church (Pathfinder 1237 341377) (Point B), which bears closer examination. Over the doorway of the south porch is a curious panel bearing the initials 'R.B.', denoting

Richard Beere, the penultimate Abbot of Glastonbury. The buttresses outside the south transept bear indentations which, according to tradition, were caused by rebel soldiers sharpening their scythes before the Battle of Sedgemoor. Inside, on the floor by the south door, is a fine brass depicting Sir Richard Sydenham of Chedzoy who died towards the end of the fifteenth century. Attention should also be paid to the splendidly carved bench ends. The rector at the time of the battle, Andrew Paschall, who seems to have discouraged involvement in the rebellion, nevertheless left an interesting account of events.

To the left of the entrance to the churchyard is a rather worn map identifying the various footpaths one may take to explore the battlefield. After viewing, turn back down Front Street, walk past Higher Road on the right and, a little further on, to the left – almost opposite the school – is a narrow track. Proceed along here. A barely discernible path off to the right leading through the fields could be difficult to negotiate. The rebels, it will be remembered, anticipated such a problem and gave Chedzoy a wide berth. Continue along the track, eventually negotiating a stile and then a gate, to emerge on to a wider track leading to Parchey and the northern outskirts of Chedzoy.

Turn right to pick up the rebel line of march. King's Sedgemoor Drain is beyond the fields to the left. Keep an eye open for a small sign on a fence by a gate, advising the rambler that for purposes of nature study one may walk across the field to the Drain. One may take this path or walk on to the T-junction, to turn left and walk down to join the very pleasant path adjoining the Drain. At this point, the rebel vanguard would have changed course, to swing towards Westonzoyland. Turn right and follow the Drain which, with its abundance of bird and plant life, is surely deserving of a more attractive nomenclature. Cross the footbridge over Chedzoy New Cut (one gate opens, the other has to be climbed) and walk on.

From here on, the walking may become tedious because of the gates to be negotiated at the end of every field. Some of the gates may be open, while others will have to be climbed, although several also possess rickety stiles. However, the area between the footbridge and the overhead cables provides what is probably the best vantage point on the public footpath system from which to view the battlefield, and it is well worth pausing here to visualize the probable rebel deployment.

Continue to follow the line of the Drain as it veers away from Westonzoyland. Eventually, a second footbridge, linking the north and south banks, appears ahead. Turn to the right here and walk through the field to join up with a well defined track at the end. Turn right and walk on, passing the rather sooty track leading to Burdenham Farm. As the footpath through the fields to Westonzoyland is unmarked, it is important to take note of the distinctive field pattern on the left. At the third field past the farm track, climb the gate and make for the far right-hand corner. Then, walk through into the next field, hugging the hedgerow on the right. It should be possible to exit from this field and turn to the right, but barbed wire ahead renders this difficult. Therefore, walk through to the adjacent field and, upon exiting, bear left. This will bring one out on to a track leading through the ruins of the main site of Westonzoyland airfield. Walk through the site and out, via the gate, turning right, on to the road linking Liney with Bussex.

Walk to Bussex Farm, where there is a mounted plan of the battle (Pathfinder 1237 355354), and straight on, up the track, towards the memorial. A sign directs the walker along a path to the right, to the memorial site (Pathfinder 1237 352357) (Point C), which lies just to the south of the Bussex Rhine's other crossing point. (Feversham's Royalist infantry would have been deployed to the right of this path.) Occasionally, visitors looking out over Lang Moor have sighted a ghostly figure, identified as Monmouth, taking flight. Others have reported seeing rebel soldiers, trying to entice the Royalist infantry over the Bussex Rhine, with cries of 'Come on over!'

One should now return to the 'To The Battlefield' sign and turn right on to the track which soon veers left on to the track servicing the sewage works. Emerging back on to the A372, turn left and walk back into Westonzoyland. Continue on into the village to see the church (Point D) which is usually kept locked, so one has to request the key. Once again, although this time in the interior, the initials of Richard Beere are in evidence. On the evening of 6 July, several hundred rebel prisoners, many fearfully wounded, were herded inside to take what rest they could on the fifteenth-century benches. When Monmouth himself was apprehended, the bells rang out.

On the way back to the starting point of the walk, one may wish to take refreshment at the appropriately named Sedgemoor Inn. Pre-dating the battle, the inn contains a framed picture depicting the battle and a framed list of its landlords, including the incumbent in 1685.

Further Explorations

Bridgwater (Landranger 182 3037) has some important points of reference for the Sedgemoor visitor. First there is the castle. All that is left of the Norman fortress is a stone archway situated on West Quay but it was here that Monmouth was proclaimed King of England for the second time. Even had the rebels intended to fortify the town against Feversham, they would have found it difficult to do so as the castle had been slighted after the Civil War. On the other hand, St Mary's Church, in St Mary Street, remains intact, with the tower from which Monmouth surveyed the Royalist camp at Westonzoyland.

Bridgwater was also home to Robert Blake, Cromwell's famous General-at-Sea. Blake, who built his reputation on holding out – alone if necessary – in sieges, distinguished himself in the defence of Bristol in July 1643, of Lyme Regis in March 1644 and of Taunton from July to December 1644. Such was the esteem in which he was held that in 1649, despite never once having been to sea, he was appointed General-at-Sea. His house in Blake Street is now the Admiral Blake Museum which has a room devoted to the Battle of Sedgemoor.

The village of Norton St Philip (Landranger 172 7756) is of interest, in part because Cromwell lodged at the George Inn in 1645, but mainly because of the engagement of 27 June, which occurred just to the north of the village. It was in the George Inn that Monmouth narrowly escaped an assassination attempt – or perhaps just a stray bullet. It is also said that here Abraham Holmes, wounded in the fray, used a meat cleaver to amputate his own mangled arm.

Glastonbury (Landranger 183 3950) is associated with many myths and legends and is as much a place of pilgrimage for the modern New Age mystic as for those whom, in centuries past, revered Glastonbury Tor as the last resting place of King Arthur and the burial place of the Holy Grail. Glastonbury Abbey, founded in AD 700, rose to greatness through the efforts of St Dunstan. It is to be doubted whether the romance of his surroundings was uppermost in Monmouth's mind when he camped there on the night of 22 June after a day of marching in heavy rain. Twenty-eight Glastonbury rebels were among those who sought shelter in the abbey grounds. On 3 July Feversham passed through, halting long enough to hang six of them from the sign of the White Hart.

Most of the settlements which accommodated Monmouth on his perambulations bear testimony to the rebels' presence. At Wells, for example, they expressed their contempt for the ceremonial by attempting to wreck the cathedral. Lead was torn from the roof for conversion into bullets and Lord Grey had to stand guard over the altar to protect it from desecration. It is said that the behaviour of the rebels in Wells marked a turning point for the cause. Only thirteen recruits – a fraction of the number Monmouth expected to attract in the town – materialized.

At Shepton Mallet (Landranger 183 6243), the reception was similarly lukewarm, just five names being added to the roster – a circumstance which might be ascribed to the arrival in the west of the Royalist army. When, on his retreat to Bridgwater, the duke paused again at Shepton Mallet to review his troops on Windsor Hill (Landranger 183 6145), he must have been alarmed at the extent to which desertions had thinned their ranks. As a result of Judge Jeffreys' deliberations, twelve would later be convicted of treason and be sentenced to die in the Market Square, now a pedestrian shopping precinct.

As already noted, the suggested battlefield walk takes one via the Westonzoyland Second World War airfield. The area was first used for flying during the 1920s and 1930s as part of anti-aircraft defence exercises which the Air Ministry organized in the summer months. By late 1940 16 Squadron, comprising Westland Lysanders had moved in, followed by 239 Squadron a year later. Throughout this period, the airfield still had grass runways. Not until 1943 was Westonzoyland upgraded and tarmac runways laid down. Thereafter, squadrons came and went until 1944 when the USAAF arrived to use the facility for D-Day preparations. After its return to the RAF, Westonzoyland became the focus of training activity until 1946, when it faced closure. There followed a further flurry of training activity in the early 1950s as part of the British response to the war in Korea. Finally, in the mid-1950s Westonzoyland accommodated Canberra aircraft, ultimately bound for Australia as part of the British Atomic Task Force. One finds it difficult to associate the sad appearance of the airfield today with its impressive pedigree.

Further Information

'Sedgemoor' – a geographical expression as opposed to a settlement – may not be readily identifiable in gazetteers. The nearest village is Westonzoyland, which lies on the A372 between Bridgwater and Langport. As already noted, a little roadside car parking space is available to the rear of the general stores.

Westonzoyland never possessed a railway station, but a bus service connects the village with Bridgwater, only 3 miles distant, so perhaps the absence of the railway has not been a great disadvantage. For details of rail services between London (Paddington) and Bridgwater, telephone 0171 262 6767. For details of National Express coach cross-country services to Bridgwater, telephone 0990 808080. For further information about bus services between Bridgwater and Westonzoyland, telephone 01823 255696.

One's interest in the battle can hardly fail to be stirred by the generous amount of readily available stimulating reading. All the standard battlefield texts contain chapters. Young and Adair's *From Hastings to Culloden* contains a succinct account, while a more florid rendering appears in Wetherell's *Fields of Fame in England and Scotland*. Seymour's *Battles in Britain 1642–1746* includes a useful aerial photograph. Of the books devoted entirely to the campaign, two in particular should be consulted:

Robin Clifton's *The Last Popular Rebellion* and David Chandler's *Sedgemoor 1685*. Clifton's detailed research is indispensable and Chandler, who manages to combine academic excellence with readability, includes reflections on his own detailed explorations of the battlefield. Also of interest is a locally produced publication, *Monmouth's West Country Rebellion of 1685* by Nigel J. Clarke, available at the Admiral Blake Museum (telephone 01278 456127 for details of opening times). Ordnance Survey maps of the area are Landranger 182 and Pathfinder 1237.

There are Tourist Information Offices in High Street, Bridgwater, as well as at the Podimore Service Area at the junction of A373 and A303, and at Sedgemoor Services on the M5. Somerset tourist services are coordinated from County Hall, Taunton (telephone 01823 255010).

12
RAF CHARMY DOWN
1940–5

Introduction

Many people, if they give the matter any consideration at all, may think of Second World War airfields as occupying, almost exclusively, the eastern half of the British Isles. To an extent, this is a justifiable point of view, for the eastern counties, in particular Lincolnshire, bore the brunt of the bombing offensive against Germany. The south west, one may be forgiven for thinking, was far removed from the main theatre of airborne operations.

As far as participation in aviation was concerned, the south west had not always been out on a limb, a notable instance being the establishment of the British & Colonial Aeroplane Company, which commenced manufacturing at Filton in 1910. Over 5,000 Bristol fighter planes were built at Filton during the First World War. Also during the First World War, a number of airfields sprang up and in the 1930s civil airports were developed to serve the major cities, such as Bristol and Plymouth.

On the outbreak of the Second World War, in the autumn of 1939, only two or three operational units existed in the south-western counties. The First World War airfield at Mount Batten near Plymouth had survived various vicissitudes in the 1920s to retain a measure of viability, and construction of a facility at St Eval, near Newquay, was under way, but there was no sense of urgency in providing airfields for what was considered to be a relatively safe area.

The fall of France in June 1940 necessitated a rapid change of strategy. Suddenly, from the relative security of operating from the French air bases, the RAF was forced to retreat back across the English Channel. The Luftwaffe moved eagerly on to their new bases and although several of them were bombed by the RAF, the fact remained that the enemy would make the most of these new forward positions to carry the war in the air to every corner of the British Isles – including the south west.

Aircraft manufacture had continued at Filton throughout the inter-war years and, during the Second World War, more than 14,000 Blenheims, Beauforts and Beaufighters were churned out. The Beaufighter, once its teething troubles were ironed out, equipped fifty-two RAF squadrons, while the Blenheim, described as a tireless workhorse, was responsible for carrying the war on to the continent in the early years of the conflict.

Bristol had welcomed the prosperity which the aircraft manufacturing industry had brought to the city but in wartime the distinct disadvantages were now driven home. If its position as a west coast seaport were sufficient to make it worthy of the Luftwaffe's attention, then its importance to the RAF rendered it doubly so. In the months between 7 September 1940 and 16 May 1941 alone, 919 tons of bombs were dropped on the city. The worst raid on the Filton works took place on 25 September 1940, and resulted in serious damage and many deaths. During the same period, Plymouth absorbed 1,228 tons of bombs, confirming the view that the west of Britain was just as vulnerable as the east. Even RAF Predannack, near Lizard Point, fell prey to Luftwaffe surprise attacks.

In fact, few airfields were ever constructed in Devon and Cornwall. Of those that were, the majority were dotted around the coastline, with the squadrons which staffed them being engaged primarily in the war against the U-Boats. At RAF Chivenor (Devon), for example, the Leigh Light (see p 140) was first used against an Italian submarine. Provision for rural Somerset and Dorset was also sparse. By far the most concentrated grouping of airfields in the south west was to the north of Salisbury, with nineteen sites reaching out over Salisbury Plain towards Swindon. While the most was certainly being made of the topographical advantages of Salisbury Plain, there still remained a need for air bases nearer to Bristol and the Severn estuary.

The Road to Charmy Down

The problem of providing airfields in the area to the west of Salisbury Plain was essentially topographical. The Mendip Hills of Somerset, their peaks rising above 1,000 ft, dominate the area to the south of Bristol, while the Cotswolds, with a marginally lower average height, stretch away to the north east. Although anything but ideal for airfield construction, it was found occasionally that this terrain could work to one's advantage. The saving grace of some of the hills to the north of Bath, for example, lay in the fact that they did not terminate in a peak. Instead, they broadened out into plateaux. One such example is that of Charmy Down, situated some 3 miles north of Bath. Whereas several plateaux in the surrounding area display a tendency towards the long and narrow, Charmy Down possesses both length and breadth. Bordered by sharp gradients on all sides, the hilltop, at its maximum no more than 700 ft in height, has an east–west span of almost 1 mile and a north–south span of a little over ⅔ mile. With careful planning, it was decided, an airfield could be constructed on Charmy Down.

Work was carried out during 1940. Three tarmac runways were constructed: the main runway, running from south-east to north-west, measured 1,450 yd; a second runway, running from south-west to north-east, measured 1,350 yd; and a short runway, north–south in direction, measured 933 yd. Although it was the practice, wherever possible, to include relatively generous safety margins to allow for pilots overshooting the runway, at Charmy Down the specifications were tight, and there was little leeway for errors of judgement either in taking off or landing.

So, in terms of the runway layout, the plan seemed to have worked, but space also had to be found for the airfield's main ancillary buildings and the dispersal sites. The main airfield site (Site No. 1) was located immediately to the west, between the perimeter road and the A46. Prominent, perhaps pre-eminent, among the buildings on Site No. 1 was the Watch Office. In common with much airfield architecture, watch offices were quite austere structures, but the Watch Office at Charmy Down was not displeasing to the eye. Brick built, with lots of window space and capped with a small observation tower, it was one of the more substantial buildings of its type built in the opening months of the war.

It was usual practice for additional communal sites to be dispersed over a wide area, but here again, everything remained quite compact. Flying began before living accommodation became available on sites to both east and west of the A46. The main communal site was Site No. 3, by Hartley Farm. In addition to the officer's quarters, the buildings included grocery stores, recreation huts and a high-level water tower. Separated from Site No. 1 by a single field was the WAAF site, which – with change of airfield use – was later converted to a communal site. Wherever possible, WAAF sites would stand in something akin to splendid isolation, on sites well away from the airmen's accommodation. An additional WAAF site was provided on the other side of the A46, with airmen's quarters on three adjacent sites. Although quite close to the main airfield site, the nature of the terrain meant that access was not quite as straightforward as one might have wished.

A final point of interest concerns the name of the airfield. It was customary for airfields to take the name of the nearest village. In this case, therefore, it might have been more appropriate to call it Swainswick, or even Tadwick or St Catherine. Only when a proposed name clashed with one already in existence was a deviation from this rule of thumb considered necessary. Perhaps Charmy Down, up on high – invisible to anyone travelling on the A46 down below – merited recognition as a community in its own right.

RAF Charmy Down 1940–1945

RAF Charmy Down began operating in November 1940 as a satellite of RAF Colerne, becoming home for 87 Squadron's night-fighter Hurricanes, which were gradually transferred from Colerne as additional accommodation at Charmy Down became available. Colerne and Charmy Down were two of many airfields which were pressed into action before completion.

The Hawker Hurricane had undertaken its maiden flight in 1935, entering service in 1937. Capable in favourable conditions of speeds in excess of 400 m.p.h. it became, with the Spitfire, Britain's saviour in the air. In its various guises of Mk I through to Mk XII, a grand total of almost 13,000 rolled off the production lines. During the Battle of Britain, the Hurricanes had acquitted themselves well, but the fighting had happened in daylight, and no one was prepared for the Luftwaffe's switch to night raids. The British response, not surprisingly, was to set up a committee. What was surprising was that this committee worked quickly to produce a report, the main recommendations of which were speedily implemented. One of the committee members, Air Vice Marshal Sholto Douglas, suggested that a number of Hurricane squadrons should be reserved specifically for night-fighting. Thus, 87 Squadron, with its distinctive black fighters, arrived at Charmy Down.

Attempts to extend the night-fighter concept to other aircraft, notably Defiants and Westland Whirlwinds, were not a success. However, one interesting expansion of night-flying work at Charmy Down involved the 'Turbinlite'. Invented by Group Captain Helmore, the Turbinlite could be fitted into the nose of night-flying aircraft to give out a strong, diffused light which would illuminate enemy bombers, enabling accompanying allied aircraft to identify and destroy them. In March 1942 night-fighter Hurricanes flew the first of several patrols in the company of a Douglas Havoc fitted with a Turbinlite. However, trials were continuing elsewhere, under the auspices of Coastal Command, with specific reference to attacks on U-Boats, with the Leigh Light, a powerful searchlight directed by ASV (Air to Surface Vessel) radar. The brain-child of Squadron Leader Leigh, a First World War pilot, the Leigh Light succeeded where the Turbinlite failed and by the beginning of 1943 the Turbinlite operations at Charmy Down had ceased.

The new year also heralded a change of use for Charmy Down, with the arrival of an Operational Training Unit, the Flight Leader School, accompanied by thirty-six Spitfires. FLS, the function of which was to give short courses in tactics, was established in January 1943, and began life at RAF Chedworth, but moved to Charmy Down shortly afterwards. During the six months which FLS spent here, some valuable tactics were developed, particularly in respect of evasive techniques for squadrons of Douglas Boston bombers. The Bostons would normally attack in groups of six, and it was found that if the leading aircraft went into a dive while aircraft two and three undertook a corkscrew manoeuvre, the aim of enemy fighter pilots would be upset. Precision timing was required but, nevertheless, the tactic quickly became standard procedure.

In August 1943 Charmy Down was allocated to the USAAF, necessitating the removal of Flight Leader School to Aston Down. Between the allocation of an airfield to the USAAF and its occupation of the premises, there was usually a gap of some months, and Charmy Down proved to be no exception, the Ninth US Air Force taking possession in February 1944. To avoid the valuable facilities remaining idle for several months, it was decided to house 2,000 RAF personnel on site temporarily. When the USAAF did eventually take over, Charmy Down was used primarily as a depot in the run-up to D-Day.

In October 1944, with its transfer back to the RAF and Flying Training Command, Charmy Down once more assumed a training role as a satellite field for RAF South Cerney, in which capacity it lived out its final period of active service.

The Aftermath

Situated near Cirencester, South Cerney had been running refresher courses for pilots since 1942 and started using the Charmy Down facility in November 1944. South Cerney survived the end of the war in Europe, training activities continuing, in one form or another, until the late 1960s.

Initially, Charmy Down was retained in its satellite capacity, on a care and maintenance basis, until such time as a decision was reached with regard to its future. At first it seemed as though a role had been found for it when in January 1946 training in glider flying began, an activity for which it appeared to be well fitted. However, this soon ceased and following a period of use as a resettlement centre, Charmy Down was finally closed.

As much as anything, its demise resulted from its unsuitability for expansion. Space had always been limited, the runways having been laid on

Many airfields never returned to their pre-war patterns of usage, retaining an aura of decay and desolation. Surviving runways and service roads are often used as hard-standing for caravan storage, with grassland offering, at best, poor grazing for cattle.

the plateau with no room to spare, while dispersal sites had been huddled together on land to the west of the A46 with relatively poor access to the airfield itself. As a potential civil airport, Charmy Down was a non-starter.

At the end of the war, many airfields were handed over to government departments to be used for storage purposes and in 1947 the Ministry of Health took over the communal sites at Charmy Down. In 1949 the site was finally closed. Its subsequent return to agricultural use has been partially successful, although its utility as farmland is hampered by the brick and concrete reminders of its past which still cling tenaciously to life.

The contribution of RAF Charmy Down to the war effort is difficult to assess. It was a small cog in a large wheel and played no less a role than dozens of similar component parts which went to make up the whole. Its success in the defence of Bristol and Bath may be questioned – the Luftwaffe was able to destroy much of historic Bath in the infamous Baedeker Raids of 1942 – but any failings must be ascribed to the technological limitations attendant upon night-fighter operations at the time.

The Walk

Distance: 6 miles (9.66 km)

At the time of writing (1995), on-going road improvements have led to some disruption of the A46 at Swainswick. On the occasion of the author's last visit, only one of three access paths to Charmy Down in the immediate area was still negotiable, and the route of the walk is not as circular in nature as one might wish. A little space for car parking is available by the telephone box on the northbound side of the old road (Pathfinder 1183 759687) (Point A), the starting point for the walk. (Care is needed in Swainswick itself as the village roads are very narrow.)

Cross the A46 and take the public footpath to the left through the copse. An alternative path to the right, through the open fields, appears to have been closed, for a reason unrelated to the roadworks. It is a steep but fairly short climb up to the Down. Bear right and as one approaches the top, a welcome yellow public footpath marker is apparent. Continue on to a stile

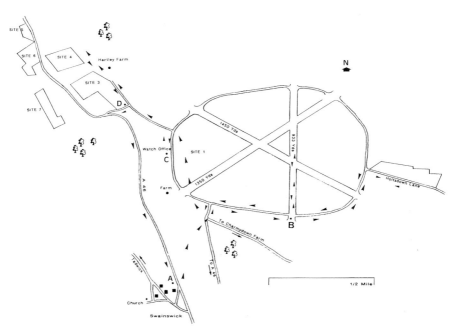

RAF Charmy Down, 1940–5

leading to an open field. Negotiate the stile and turn left. Cross the field, entering the next field by the gap in the wall. Head for the far right-hand corner and emerge, via another stile, on to a single-track road. Turn left and take the farm track with the barn on the left-hand side (Pathfinder 1183 760695). This track, on which were once sited two aircraft hangars, leads out on to the airfield itself which is adorned with a bewildering array of public footpath signs.

Turn right to follow the southern airfield perimeter path. Note the air raid shelters, virtually the only surviving buildings on the southern portion of the site. The public footpath a little way ahead, branching off to the left (Pathfinder 1183 763696), but not indicated on the OS map, follows the course of the short runway (Point C). Continue straight on past the footpath on the right (a circuitous route down to the A46) and on to the south-east corner of one of the two main runways (Pathfinder 1183 767696). Pass through the gate into the next field where, a short distance on, the path veers sharply to the right on to what was once (before the construction of the airfield) Holtsdown Lane. On the left-hand side are the foundations of barrack huts, latrines and stores. Further on is the only structure left standing on this site: a machine-gun test butt (Pathfinder 1183 771698). It is now necessary to retrace one's steps back to Point C.

Walk a little way up the short runway. Critics will point out that, in common with many old airfield sites and, indeed, battlefields in general, there is very little to see. This is true, but the dereliction often contributes to the ambience of the sites. The work involved in filling in the missing details and picturing the ground as it used to be, the focus of urgent activity, is all part of the fascination of this type of exploration.

Return to the perimeter path and continue to the track by the barn and on to the single-track road. Immediately to the right is a signposted public footpath. Follow it through the trees out into the field and, hugging the right-hand edge, continue through to the next field. Some care is needed as fencing rope has been used to define the field boundaries. Flexible and easy to negotiate, it is difficult to see in poor light. This section of the public footpath system does require adequate marking. However, when the fields open up on the right, continue to walk straight ahead, to emerge on to the area defined on the original airfield plan as Site No. 1. Here, amid a few dilapidated buildings, is a miraculous survival of an ever-increasing rarity: the airfield watch tower (Pathfinder 1167 755800) (Point D).

Continue straight ahead down the track towards the farm. On the left is a road leading down to the A46 (Point E). Note the pink building on the corner (Pathfinder 1167 752703). Originally the Officers' Mess, part of Communal Site 3, it shows how airfield buildings other than hangars may

The watch tower at Charmy Down. Note the replacement window frames on the top level. After the war, the housing shortage led to the conversion for domestic use of many airfield buildings – often not dissimilar to housing created via the post-war prefabrication programme. Of rather more substance, the watch towers had greater potential for development, although exposed situations coupled with a profusion of windows led to extremes of temperature.

still be adapted for modern usage. As such, it forms a stark contrast to the dilapidation of the rest of the architecture. The path leads directly past the farm, and then on into the fields, hugging the left-hand boundary. Amid the ruins, one may discern a storehouse (Pathfinder 1167 751704); the decontamination centre (Pathfinder 1167 750705); dining room (Pathfinder 1167 749704) and high-level water tower (Pathfinder 1167 748704). An open field separates this site from Communal Site 4, of which little survives beyond the ablutions, latrines and drying rooms (Pathfinder 1167 748706).

Although it is possible to continue along the footpath to gain access to the A46, it is preferable to retrace one's steps to join the road by the track at Point E. Walking alongside the A46 is fairly comfortable, although it is necessary to cross over two or three times to use the wider grass verge. By joining via the track at Point E, the A46 section is substantially reduced. And to the west one can still enjoy panoramic views over the downs. Continue along the A46, back to the starting point.

Further Explorations

Charmy Down was quite a compact airfield, with its twelve sites grouped together on either side of the A46. It is possible to make a more comprehensive survey although the limitations of the public footpath system to the west of the A46, coupled with the destruction of nearly all the buildings, render it feasible only for the most dedicated explorer.

The location of the site sick quarters is easily identified, just past the Tadwick turn-off on the A46 (Pathfinder 1167 746709). The location of sites 5, 6, 7 and 8, running parallel with the A46, may be identified by the track running from Pathfinder 1167 746707 to 749701). Of these, Site 6 (Pathfinder 1167 746707) has fared best over the years, with the survival of a handful of buildings, which may be viewed from the public footpath linking the A46 with Tadwick.

Of the outermost sites, the radio stations, very little trace remains. The VHF Transmitting Station was situated at Shapland's Farm, Cold Ashton (Pathfinder 1167 74757245), and the Receiving Station was located on Henley Hill (Pathfinder 1167 749715). Note the service road; the Homing Station was sited on Nimlet Hill (Pathfinder 1167 743712).

Unfortunately, there are few opportunities for anyone wishing to explore more airfields in the area. The nearest site is at North Stoke or, more accurately, on the ground occupied by Lansdown Racecourse (Pathfinder 1183 718688). There had been a racecourse on the spot before the war and in 1943 it was decided to adapt it to serve as a relief landing ground for the training unit at Castle Combe (Landranger 173 8576). As the racecourse buildings were deemed satisfactory for use, very little new building work, beyond runway construction, was carried out, which is why there is almost no evidence of wartime usage to be seen today.

Castle Combe airfield itself struggled along with grass runways for some years. One of the prerequisites for an airfield was adequate site drainage, but almost continuous waterlogging here meant that for lengthy periods, flying became impossible. The situation was never fully resolved, and was only marginally improved after the laying of metal track runways. The perimeter track proved more durable and, in later years, was considered suitable for use as a motor racing circuit, which led to the preservation of several main airfield site buildings, which in all probability would otherwise have been lost. Even so, the scars left by the airfield upon the local landscape were not so severe as to preclude Castle Combe village subsequently winning awards in best-kept village competitions.

Colerne (Landranger 173 8071), like its neighbours Charmy Down and North Stoke, occupied a plateau. It was part of the RAF airfield expansion scheme, embarked upon in the 1930s as a result of a well founded fear of Germany's covert re-armament programme. From 1940 to 1945 Colerne was put to many uses: as a training field; as an operational base giving fighter cover to the Bristol area; as an assembly area for fighters; and as a base for squadrons on shipping reconnaissance duties. Surviving the post-war closure programme, Colerne continued in service with the RAF until the mid-1970s. A glance at the Ordnance Survey map is enough to indicate the extent to which the airfield dominated the life of the village of Colerne, which itself occupies the south-eastern corner of the plateau. Although the site, circumscribed by minor roads, is worth seeing, the general point might be made that although one might imagine that airfields which survived the war either to continue in service with the RAF, or to be used as civil aerodromes, would be rich in reminders of the past, this is not always the case, with the obliteration of original features resulting from the need for expansion and modernization of facilities.

Further Information

Shrouded in woodland, Charmy Down lies off the A46, 2½ miles to the north of Bath. At the time of writing (1995), the portion of the A46 adjoining Swainswick – the nearest village – is in the throes of a road improvement scheme which, inevitably, has led to temporary delays for motorists. However, car parking space by the telephone booth on the northbound carriageway should remain accessible.

The nearest railway station is situated at Bath. For details of services between London (Paddington) and Bath Spa, telephone 0171 262 6767. For details of Cross Country connections, telephone 01225 464446. Bath is also accessible by National Express coach. For details of services, telephone 0990 808080. For details of local connecting bus services, call 0117 955 5111.

Further reading is available in Chris Ashworth's *Action Stations 5: Military Airfields of the South-West* and in Jonathan Falconer's *RAF Fighter Airfields of World War 2*. Visitors to RAF Charmy Down are advised to purchase a copy of the official airfield plan, produced by *After the Battle* magazine in association with the RAF Museum, Hendon. Contact *After the Battle* magazine at Church House, Church Street, London E15 3JA.

Ordnance Survey maps for the area are Landranger 172 and Pathfinders 1183 and 1167, both of which are required.

FURTHER READING

Place of publication given only if outside London.

General background reading:
Churchill, Winston S., *A History of the English Speaking Peoples: The Birth of Britain* (Cassell & Co. Ltd, 1956)
Churchill, Winston S., *A History of the English Speaking Peoples: The New World* (Cassell & Co. Ltd, 1956)

For more detailed background reading, see:
Adair, John, *Roundhead General: A Military Biography of Sir William Waller* (MacDonald and Co. Ltd, 1969)
Adam, R.J., *A Conquest of England: The Coming of the Normans* (Hodder & Stoughton, 1965)
Barlow, Frank, *The Feudal Kingdom 1042–1216* (Longman, 1988)
Clarendon, Earl of, *The History of the Great Rebellion* (Oxford University Press, 1967)
Coward, Barry, *The Stuart Age 1603–1714* (Longman, 1994)
Fisher, D.J.V., *The Anglo-Saxon Age 400–1042* (Longman, 1973)
Keynes, Simon and Lapidge, Michael (eds), *Asser's Life of King Alfred* (Penguin, 1983)
Labarge, Margaret Wade, *Simon de Montfort* (Eyre & Spottiswoode, Andover, 1962)
Whitlock, Ralph, *Warrior Kings of Saxon England* (Moonraker Press, Bradford-on-Avon, 1977)
Wilkinson, Bertie, *The Later Middle Ages 1216–1485* (Longman, 1969)

For reading relating to the Wars of the Roses, the following are recommended:
Barber, Richard (ed), *The Pastons: a family in the Wars of the Roses* (Penguin, 1984)
Kendall, Paul Murray, *Warwick the Kingmaker* (Allen & Unwin, 1957)
Lander, J.R., *The Wars of the Roses* (Alan Sutton Publishing Ltd, Stroud, 1990)
Wise, Terence, *The Wars of the Roses* (Osprey Publishing, 1983)

For reading relating to the English Civil War, the following are recommended:

Ashley, M., *The English Civil War* (Alan Sutton Publishing Ltd, Stroud, 1990)

Downing, T., and Millman, M., *Civil War* (Collins & Brown, 1991)

Firth, C.H., *Cromwell's Army* (Greenhill Books, 1992)

Hibbert, Christopher, *Cavaliers and Roundheads: The English at War 1642–1649* (HarperCollins, 1993)

Kenyon, John, *The Civil Wars of England* (Weidenfeld & Nicolson, 1988)

Wedgewood, C.V., *The King's War 1641–47* (Penguin, 1983)

For accounts of specific battles discussed in the text, see:

Adair, John, *Cheriton 1644: The Campaign & The Battle* (Roundwood Press, Kineton, 1973)

Atkin, Malcolm and Laughlin, Wayne, *Gloucester and the Civil War: A City Under Siege* (Alan Sutton Publishing Ltd, Stroud, 1992)

Chandler, David, *Sedgemoor 1685* (Anthony Mott Ltd, 1985)

Clarke, Nigel J., *Monmouth's West Country Rebellion of 1685* (Nigel J. Clarke Publications, Lyme Regis)

Clifton, Robin, *The Last Popular Rebellion* (Maurice Temple Smith, 1984)

Edwards, Graham, *The Battle of Langport* (Langport & District Historic Company, Langport, 1995)

Frampton, D., and Garnham, P., *The Forlorn Hope Guide to the Battle of Newbury 1643* (Partizan Press, Leigh-on-Sea)

Furneaux, Rupert, *Conquest 1066* (Secker & Warburg, 1966)

Gravett, Christopher, *Hastings, 1066: The Fall of Saxon England* (Osprey Publishing Ltd, 1994)

Hammond, P.W., *The Battles of Barnet and Tewkesbury* (Alan Sutton Publishing, Stroud, 1993)

Morris, Robert, *The First Battle of Newbury 1643* (Stuart Press, Bristol, 1993)

Morris, Robert, *The Battles of Lansdown and Roundway 1643* (Stuart Press, Bristol, 1993)

Moulder, Bob, *Western Wonders: The Battles of Lansdown and Roundway Down 1643* (Keep Wargaming, 1993)

For general accounts of British battles, see:

Ashworth, Chris, *Action Stations: Military Airfields of the South-West* (Patrick Stephens, Wellingborough, 1982)

Baker, Anthony, *A Battlefield Atlas of the English Civil War* (Ian Allan Ltd, 1986)

Barrett, C.R.B., *Battles & Battlefields in England* (A.D. Innes & Co., 1896)

Bennett, Martyn, *Traveller's Guide to the Battlefields of the English Civil War* (Webb & Bower, Exeter, 1990)

Brooke, Richard, *Visits to Fields of Battle in England in the Fifteenth Century* (John Russell Smith, 1857)

Burne, Alfred H., *The Battlefields of England* (Methuen & Co. Ltd, 1950)

Burne, Alfred H., *More Battlefields of England* (Methuen & Co. Ltd, 1952)

Fairbairn, Neil, *A Traveller's Guide to the Battlefields of Britain* (Evans Brothers, 1983)

Green, Howard, *Guide to the Battlefields of Britain & Ireland* (Constable & Co., 1973)

Kinross, John, *The Battlefields of Britain* (David & Charles, Newton Abbot, 1979)

Newman, P.R., *Atlas of the English Civil War* (Croom Helm, Beckenham, 1985)

Rogers, Colonel H.C.B., *Battles and Generals of the Civil Wars 1642–1651* (Seeley Service & Co. Ltd, 1968)

Seymour, William, *Battles in Britain 1066–1547* (Sidgwick & Jackson, 1975)

Seymour, William, *Battles in Britain 1642–1746* (Sidgwick & Jackson, 1975)

Smith, David J., *Britain's Military Airfields 1939–45* (Patrick Stephens, Wellingborough, 1989)

Smurthwaite, David, *The Complete Guide to the Battlefields of Britain* (Michael Joseph Ltd, 1993)

Warner, Philip, *British Battlefields: The South* (Osprey Publishing Ltd, 1972)

Wedgewood, C.V., *Civil War Battlefields* (BBC)

Wetherell, J.E., *Fields of Fame in England and Scotland* (MacMillan, Toronto, 1923)

Young, Peter and Adair, John, *From Hastings to Culloden* (Roundwood Press, Kineton, 1979)

Young, Peter and Emberton, Wilfrid, *Sieges of the Great Civil War* (Bell & Hyman, 1978)

For general guides to the counties covered by this volume, see:

Gaunt, Peter, *The Cromwellian Gazetteer* (Alan Sutton Publishing Ltd, Stroud, 1992)

Mee, Arthur, *The King's England: Sussex* (Hodder & Stoughton Ltd, 1964)

——, *The King's England: Essex* (Hodder & Stoughton Ltd, 1966)

——, *The King's England: Hampshire* (Hodder & Stoughton Ltd, 1967)

——, *The King's England: Somerset* (Hodder & Stoughton Ltd, 1968)

——, *The King's England: Berkshire* (Hodder & Stoughton Ltd, 1964)

——, *The King's England: Hertfordshire* (Hodder & Stoughton Ltd, 1965)

——, *The King's England: Gloucestershire* (Hodder & Stoughton Ltd, 1966)

For an excellent all-round introduction to walking and rambling, see:

Westacott, H.D., *The Walker's Handbook* (Oxford Illustrated Press, Yeovil, 1980)

INDEX OF PLACES

Aldbourne 89
Aldermaston 92
Alresford 100, 101
Alton 100, 108
Arundel 100
Ashdown v, 1–11 *passim*
Aston Down 141
Athelney 120
Axminster 124
Aynho 87

Barnet 50–62 *passim*
Barnstaple 116
Basing 5, 99, 108, 109
Basingstoke 99, 108
Bath 65, 66, 70, 73, 116, 124, 138, 139, 142
Battle 31–6 *passim*
Beauworth 107
Berkhamsted 31, 60
Bicester 87
Bierton 87
Boreham 21
Boroughbridge 60
Bosworth v, 50, 58
Boxford 97
Brackley 39, 87
Braddock Down 63
Bradford-upon-Avon 65, 124
Bradwell-on-Sea 21
Bramdean 101
Bridgwater 112, 114, 115, 116, 122–36 *passim*
Bridport 123
Bristol 65, 69, 73, 75, 77, 112, 117, 124, 127, 137, 138, 142, 147
Burford 89
Burrow Bridge 113, 120

Castle Combe 146
Chard 65, 124
Charmy Down 137–47 *passim*
Chatteris 14

Chedworth 141
Chedzoy 126, 127, 131, 132
Cheltenham 84, 88, 89
Cheriton v, 99–110 *passim*, 116
Chieveley 97
Chippenham 7, 69
Chipping Norton 88
Chivenor 138
Christchurch 105
Cirencester 89, 141
Clevedon 73
Colchester 21, 22
Cold Ashton 73, 146
Colerne 140, 146, 147
Compton 7, 9, 10, 11
Coventry 52
Crewkerne 112
Cricklade 89
Cropredy Bridge 105
Croydon 42
Culloden 122

Dartmouth 50
Deddington 88
Devizes 69, 70
Doncaster 117
Dorchester 129, 130
Dover 31
Dunbar 60
Dyrham Park 72

Eastbourne 48
East Meon 101
Edgehill v
Edington 7
Ely 16, 21
Empingham 60
Evesham 44, 89
Exeter 130

Farnham 100, 105
Felstead 21
Filton 137, 138
Fletching 40, 158
Frome 124

Glasgow 123
Glastonbury 124, 134
Gloucester vi, 37, 39, 75–86 *passim*, 87, 88, 89, 114
Glynde 48
Grendon Underwood 87

Hampstead Norreys 11
Hamstead Marshall 70
Hastings v, vi, 25, 30, 31, 34, 35
Hempsted 84
Hermitage 97
Herstmonceux 34, 35
Hertford 60
Hexham 52
Heybridge 14
High Ham 120
Highnam 85
Hinton Ampner 101
Hoddesdon 123
Huish Episcopi 117
Hull 52
Hungerford 73

Ilchester 113, 120
Ilminster 120, 121
Ipswich 14
Isle Abbots 114

Kenilworth 31, 44
Keynsham 124
Kingston 40
Kintbury 90

Langport 111–21 *passim*
Lansdown v, 63–74 *passim*, 105, 146
Lechlade 89
Leicester 38, 40
Lewes v, 37–49 *passim*
Lindisfarne 2, 21
London 6, 14, 17, 27, 31, 39, 40, 52, 53, 54, 56, 60, 75, 89, 92, 99, 105, 124, 126, 128, 130

Long Load 113
Low Ham 120
Lyme Regis 105, 123, 134

Maldon 12–23 *passim*
Marlborough 9
Marshfield 66, 68, 73
Marston Moor v
Monkton Farleigh 65
Muchelney 120

Naseby v, 111
Naunton 85, 88
Newark 101, 117
Newbury vi, 87–98 *passim*
Newmarket 123
Newquay 137
Northampton 39
Northey Island 14–23 *passim*
North Stoke 146
Norton St Philip 124, 134
Nottingham 3, 40, 52

Odiham 109
Offham 41, 42, 46
Over 84
Oxford 39, 88, 91, 96, 105

Painswick 85
Pensford 124
Petersfield 100, 101
Petherton 113
Pevensey 25, 26, 27, 34, 35
Plymouth 137
Poitiers 60
Pontefract 52
Portsmouth 56

Predannack 138
Prestbury 88
Prestonpans 60, 122
Pucklechurch 73

Ravenspur 52
Reading 3, 5, 97, 105
Rochester 18, 40
Romsey 100
Rotherham 13
Rouen 25
Roundway Down 63, 64, 69,
    105

St Albans 39, 50, 51, 61
St Eval 137
St Valery 25, 26
Salisbury 65, 138
Seaford 48
Sedgemoor v, 122–36 *passim*
Shepton Mallet 124, 125,
    134
Sheriffmuir 122
Somerton 112, 114
Sourton Down 63
Southampton 14, 100
South Cerney 141
Stamford Bridge 27
Stanton Drew 73
Stockbridge 105
Stockcross 97
Stoke Field 50
Stow-on-the-Wold 88, 89
Stratton 63, 65
Sutton Veny 7
Swainswick 129, 143
Swindon 89, 138

Tadwick 139, 146
Taunton 111, 113, 114, 124,
    129, 130
Taynton 85
Tetbury 85
Tettenhall 12
Tewkesbury 50, 56, 57, 89
Tibberton 85
Tichborne 101, 102
Tonbridge 40
Towcester 12
Towton v

Upton-upon-Severn 89

Waddesdon 87
Wallingford 31
Waltham 27, 30
Wantage 10
Warnford 101
Wells 65, 130, 134
Westonzoyland   124–35
        passim
Weymouth 56
Wilton 6
Wimborne 6
Winchcombe 85
Winchester 48, 99, 100, 101,
    104, 105
Windsor 38
Winterbourne 97
Worcester 65, 89, 105

Yeovil 113
Yeovilton 120
York 3, 13, 27, 52, 54,
    105

INDEX OF PERSONS

Alfred the Great (King of the
    English) v, 2–11 *passim*,
    12, 13, 16, 75, 119,
    120
Appleyard, Colonel Matthew
    102, 107
Argyll, Archibald Campbell,
    9th Earl of 123, 125
Artorius 1

Asser, Bishop of Sherborne
    4, 5, 6, 7
Aston, Colonel Sir Arthur
    90
Athelstan (King of the
    English) 13, 16
Atkyns, Captain Richard 67,
    68, 72
Audley, James 44

Aurelianus, Ambrosius 1

Bagsec 4, 5
Beere, Richard, Abbot of
    Glastonbury 132, 133
Berksted, Stephen, Bishop of
    Winchester 43
Blake, Robert 134
Boadicea 22, 61

Bolle, Colonel Richard 108
Bovill, Major 104
Britnoth 14, 15, 16, 21
Buffet, Richard 125
Burghill, Colonel Robert 65, 66
Byron, Sir John 69, 90

Carnarvon, Robert Dormer, 1st Earl of 65, 66, 67, 91
Charles I 48, 63, 65, 79, 80, 84, 89, 90, 96, 97, 105, 111, 112, 117
Charles II 21, 81, 122, 123
Charles the Bold, Duke of Burgundy 52
Chudleigh, Sir James 63
Churchill, John (later Duke of Marlborough) 124, 127
Clarence, George, Duke of 52
Commeline, James 82
Compton, Sir Francis 126, 127
Crawford, Earl of 69, 108
Cromwell, Oliver 21, 60, 61, 65, 81, 85, 86, 96, 97, 108, 109, 116, 117, 134

Desborough, Major John 115
Digby, Colonel George, Lord 93, 117

Edgar, the Atheling 31
Edmund (King of the English) 13, 73
Edmund 'Crouchback', King of Sicily 37
Edred (King of the English) 13
Edward IV 51–62 passim
Edward, Prince of Wales (later Edward I) 38, 40, 41, 42, 46, 47
Edward the Confessor (King of the English) 24
Edward the Elder (King of the English) 12, 13, 14, 16, 20
Edward the Martyr (King of the English) 13
Edwin, Earl 30, 31
Edwin, King of Northumbria 2

Edwy (King of the English) 13
Egbert, King of Northumbria 6
Egbert, King of Wessex 2, 3
Eleanor of Provence 38, 44
Elfrida 13
Elizabeth Woodville 51
Eric Bloodaxe 13
Essex, Robert Devereux, 3rd Earl of 80, 87–98 passim, 105
Ethelbald, King of Mercia 2
Ethelbald, King of Wessex 3
Ethelbert, King of Wessex 3
Ethelfleda, Queen of Mercia 12
Ethelred, King of Wessex 3, 4, 5, 6
Ethelred II, the Unready (King of the English) 13, 16, 17, 18, 24
Ethelwald, son of Ethelred I 12
Ethelwulf, King of Wessex 3
Ethelwulf, son of Ethelred, King of Wessex 12
Exeter, Henry Holland, 3rd Duke of 53, 55

Fairfax, Sir Thomas 22, 60, 111–21 passim
Falkland, Julius Cary, 3rd Viscount 91, 92, 95
Fergeant, Alan, Count 28
Ferguson, Robert 123
Feversham, Louis Duras, Earl of 124–8, 133, 134
Fielding, Colonel Richard 97
Fiennes, Nathaniel 61
Fiennes, Sir Roger de 34
Fitzwilliams, Thomas 82
Fleetwood, Colonel Charles 113
Fleury, Captain Raoul 104
Floyd, Captain Euble 104
Fortesque, Major Richard 90, 91, 93
Forth, Patrick Ruthven, 1st Earl of 101, 102, 103
Foulkes, John 125
Freeman, John 84

Gerrard, Colonel Charles 90

Gloucester, Gilbert de Clare, Earl of 39, 41, 44, 47
Godric, son of Odda 16
Godwin, Earl 24
Goring, Colonel George, 1st Baron 96, 111–21 passim
Grafton, Henry Fitzroy, 1st Duke of 124
Grenville, Sir Bevil 63, 67, 70, 72
Grey of Warke, Lord 123, 124, 127, 128, 134
Grey, Sir John 51
Guthrun 7
Gwynne, Captain John 91

Halfdan 4
Harcus, Lieutenant James 79
Harold II (King of the English) 24–36 passim
Hastings, Henry de 41
Hastings, William, 1st Baron 53, 54
Helmore, Group Captain 140
Hemois, Robert, Count of 24
Hengist 1
Henrietta Maria 93
Henry II 75
Henry III 37–49 passim, 75
Henry VI 50, 53, 56, 61
Hertford, William Seymour, Marquess of 63, 65, 69, 70
Hesilrige, Sir Arthur 63, 64, 65, 67, 103, 107
Holmes, Abraham 123, 125, 129
Hopton, Lieutenant Colonel Edward 102
Hopton, Sir Ralph 63–74 passim, 99–110 passim

James II 122, 124, 130
Jeffreys, George, 1st Baron v, 129, 130, 134
John 37

Kingston, Anthony 85

Lambert, Major General John 48
Leigh, Squadron Leader 140

Leighton, Lieutenant Colonel 102
Leven, Alexander Leslie, 1st Earl of 82, 100
Lisle, Sir George 21, 22, 96, 101
Llewelyn II of Gwynedd 37
Louis IX, King of France 38, 43
Louis XI, King of France 52
Louis XIV, King of France 122
Lucas, Sir Charles 22
Lunsford, Lieutenant Colonel Henry 73

Manchester, Edward Montagu, 2nd Earl of 96, 97
Margaret of Anjou 51, 52, 56, 57
Massey, Lieutenant Colonel Edward 77–86 passim, 112, 113, 114
Matilda 24
Matthews, Edward 125
Maurice, Prince 64, 65, 66, 68, 69, 77, 89, 96, 105
Middleton, Colonel John 88, 90, 93
Monmouth, James Scott, Duke of 121, 122–36 passim
Montague, John Neville, Marquis of 52, 53, 55, 56
Montfort, Henry de 39, 41, 42
Montfort, Peter de 39
Montfort, Simon de, Earl of Leicester v, 35, 37–49 passim
Montfort, Simon de (the Younger) 39
Montgomery, Roger de 28
Montrose, James Graham, 5th Earl and 1st Marquess of 112, 116

Morcar, Earl of 30, 31
Morley, Colonel Herbert 48
Mortain, Robert de 60
Mortimer, Roger 39, 44

Neville, Anne 56
Neville, George, Archbishop of York 53, 56
Neville, Thomas, 'Bastard of Fauconberg' 56
Newcastle, William Cavendish, 1st Earl and 1st Marquess of 105

Offa, King of Mercia 2
Oglethorpe, Colonel Theophilus 124, 128
Oswald, King of Northumbria 2
Oxford, John de Vere, 13th Earl of 52–6, 59

Pembroke, Jasper Tudor, Earl of 52
Penda, King of Mercia 2
Porter, Lieutenant General George 114
Pury, Thomas 85
Pym, John 87, 99

Ragnald 13
Ramsay, Sir James 88
Robartes, Colonel, 3rd Baron 90, 93
Robert, Duke of Normandy 82
Rupert, Prince, of the Rhine, 61, 73, 77, 88, 90, 91, 92, 93, 95, 97, 101, 105, 111, 112, 116, 117

Segrave, Nicholas de 41, 42
Skippon, Major General Philip 90, 91, 93, 96
Slingsby, Sir Arthur 116
Slingsby, Lieutenant Colonel Walter 66, 104

Somerset, Edmund Beaufort, 4th Duke of 56, 57
Springate, Colonel Sir William 91
Stamford, Henry Grey, 1st Earl of 63
Stapleton, General Sir Philip 87, 90, 91, 92, 93
Stephen 35, 44
Stowell, Sir Edward 104, 107
Svein Forkbeard 17

Thompson, Colonel 104
Tryggvason, Olaf 14, 17
Tucker, Lieutenant Colonel 91

Vavasour, Colonel Sir William 79, 90, 91, 93
Voltigern 1

Wade, Nathaniel 123, 124, 125, 128
Waller, Major General Sir William 64–74 passim, 77, 85, 96, 97, 99–110 passim
Warbeck, Perkin 50
Warenne, William de 45, 46
Warwick, Richard Neville, 14th Earl of 51–62 passim
Weldon, Colonel Ralph 112
Wentworth, Lady Henrietta 123
West, Lieutenant Colonel 91
White, William 82
William I, Duke of Normandy 22, 24–36 passim, 75, 82
William II, William Rufus 35
Wilmot, Henry, 2nd Viscount 69, 70, 88
Wyndham, Sir Hugh 116
Wyntour, Sir John 77

York, Richard, Duke of 61